MBA BEFORE COLLEGE

Why Every College Student Needs to Start a Business and Learn MBA Principles Now

AILEEN YI FAN

BALBOA
PRESS
A DIVISION OF HAY HOUSE

Copyright © 2018 Aileen Yi Fan.

All rights reserved. No part of this book may be used or reproduced by any means, graphic, electronic, or mechanical, including photocopying, recording, taping or by any information storage retrieval system without the written permission of the author except in the case of brief quotations embodied in critical articles and reviews.

This book is a work of non-fiction. Unless otherwise noted, the author and the publisher make no explicit guarantees as to the accuracy of the information contained in this book and in some cases, names of people and places have been altered to protect their privacy.

Balboa Press books may be ordered through booksellers or by contacting:

Balboa Press
A Division of Hay House
1663 Liberty Drive
Bloomington, IN 47403
www.balboapress.com
1 (877) 407-4847

Because of the dynamic nature of the Internet, any web addresses or links contained in this book may have changed since publication and may no longer be valid. The views expressed in this work are solely those of the author and do not necessarily reflect the views of the publisher, and the publisher hereby disclaims any responsibility for them.

The author of this book does not dispense medical advice or prescribe the use of any technique as a form of treatment for physical, emotional, or medical problems without the advice of a physician, either directly or indirectly. The intent of the author is only to offer information of a general nature to help you in your quest for emotional and spiritual well-being. In the event you use any of the information in this book for yourself, which is your constitutional right, the author and the publisher assume no responsibility for your actions.

Any people depicted in stock imagery provided by Getty Images are models, and such images are being used for illustrative purposes only. Certain stock imagery © Getty Images.

Print information available on the last page.

ISBN: 978-1-9822-0964-3 (sc)
ISBN: 978-1-9822-0962-9 (hc)
ISBN: 978-1-9822-0963-6 (e)

Library of Congress Control Number: 2018909231

Balboa Press rev. date: 10/16/2018

DEDICATION

To William, Ian, and Amy; you inspire me to be the best version of myself every day.

To all my teachers who showed up in my life at the perfect time when I was ready, I am forever grateful.

To the Universe, thank you for this wonderful life despite all the ups and downs. We are never separated. Love forever.

ACKNOWLEDGMENTS

I want to say thank you to all my teachers, mentors, authors and entrepreneurs who graciously shared their experience and wisdom through their teachings and writings. You taught me the power of working towards a noble mission. You changed my life forever and for the better.

To my favorite teachers Dr. Wayne W. Dyer and Louis Hay. You continue to inspire me even when you transitioned to heaven. Thank you for helping me to find me.

To Jack Welch and Suzy Welch, thank you for founding the Jack Welch Management Institute and sharing your business wisdom openly and unselfishly. To Andrea Backman, I am grateful to have you as my Dean. You are an inspiration.

CONTENTS

Acknowledgments vii
Chapter 1   Why Learn MBA Concepts Before College? 1
Chapter 2   Leadership: Inspiration, Edge and Adaptability...... 11
Chapter 3   Communication: Inform, Inspire,
            Persuade and Engage 23
Chapter 4   People Management: The Right
            People for Your Success 39
Chapter 5   Financial Management: Learn the Language of
            Business 53
Chapter 6   Marketing: Getting People to Buy What You Sell 67
Chapter 7   Operations Management: Getting Things Done
            Most Efficiently 91
Chapter 8   Managerial Economics: Making Decisions in the
            Face of Constraints 107
Chapter 9   Strategy: A Customized Playbook to Win 125
Chapter 10 Leading Change: Leader's Ability to Drive
            Change and Culture 143
Chapter 11 Entrepreneurship: How to Start Your Business..... 153
Chapter 12 Capstone: Leading as a CEO and a Business
            Owner 179
About the Author 187

CHAPTER 1
WHY LEARN MBA CONCEPTS BEFORE COLLEGE?

"We believe each child has a gift that can change the world in a profound way."
—Laura A. Sandefer, Co-founder of Acton Academy and author

All of us have inherited gifts and the potential to succeed on our own terms. I hope this book can plant a seed for high school and college students who want to live purposeful lives, even embarking on their own hero's journey to "change the world in a profound way." The earlier we take charge of our own lives, the more likely we are to make a meaningful contribution to the world. We are intrinsically happier and more peaceful when we live purposeful, authentic, and fulfilling lives.

I wrote this book for my children to teach them what I have learned in my MBA program. During the three years I studied in the online executive MBA program at the Jack Welch Management Institute, I frequently had blissful "aha moments" in learning knowledge and wisdom from Jack Welch, his professors, the world's leading CEOs on our Experts of Practice panel, and from the business books I read. Those frequent eureka moments sparked many insights and discoveries.

I also reflected on the seven different companies I worked for throughout my career, from a Fortune 50 global company to a small startup, and recognized why some of them were successful, while others were failing. I realized that most businesses failed because of people-related problems: failure of leadership, hiring the wrong people, failing to manage cash flow, failing to understand customers, failing to anticipate disruptions, and failing to adapt to change. As the old saying goes, "Businesses don't fail, people fail businesses."

I often shared my learning with my husband William, and he'd reply, "We need to teach our children and let them know this wisdom now before they get into college and business. That's your best return for the investment in the MBA program." Initially I neglected his advice until one day I "woke up" while listening to my favorite marketing luminary Seth Godin on Dave Ramsey's podcast. Godin said that every student should start a business during his or her four years at college.

Then the messages kept coming. While I was watching Louise Hay's film *You Can Heal Your Life*, I became totally mesmerized by the message from Doreen Virtue, the author and motivational speaker. She said that we are entering the time of manifestation and cooperation, a time during which people will stop going to jobs that don't matter, stop making meaningless objects that do not matter, and stop spending money on things because they feel empty inside. We will be following our personal passions, working together on our collective passions and in the process adding more meaning to all our lives.

I follow many successful entrepreneurs and media-preneurs—those who find their success via online and social media—through their books, blogs, videos, and business podcasts. Doreen Virtue's theme has been often repeated: in order for us to fulfill our passion and add meaning to our lives in this new age, we must find ways to lead ourselves from within. One of the most obvious ways to do this is to start our own businesses, big or small, for profit or non-profit, to make a difference in the world, instead of working for others in low energy jobs.

I decided to teach my then 12-year-old son Ian and 10-year-old daughter Amy the leadership, business, and people management principles taught in my MBA program. I wanted them to have the knowledge and tools so that when they start their own businesses, they will be wiser, make good business and people decisions, and reduce or avoid the same mistakes others made. Even if they did not understand all the principles at that young age with no real-life experience, I wanted them to know the tools and wisdom that exist. Once they are aware of these, they can continue their development on their own or with the help of mentors. Kids have so much brain capacity that when they want to learn, they can learn at an amazing rate.

My career transformation. Both my parents worked as mechanical engineers, staying with one employer until retirement. My parents, schools and society at large conditioned me to get good scores at school, find a safe job, raise a family, and work for others till retirement.

I worked hard to be a straight-A student, earned that safe engineering degree and found my dream job upon graduation with a global company. I really wanted to "marry" my employer and stay employed "happily ever after." But the business world was changing rapidly. My first employer was a Fortune 50 company, once one of the biggest, most successful and admired companies in the world, recognized as one of the founders of Silicon Valley. However, the company changed five CEOs during the decade after the founders passed away. Company culture and brand deteriorated, earning unfortunate attention in the news for such as topics as "the biggest layoffs of the 21st century."

After going through the agony of a spinoff and the acquisition of my business division, I moved on to work for several publicly-traded companies and small startups, some successful, some not. I gradually learned that leadership decisions matter so much that they can make or break a business, no matter how big or small. I had lost jobs due to various mergers and acquisitions or, in one case, when a seemingly well-funded startup ran out of cash.

I had followed the path that society expected of me until I got a wakeup call at age 43 when I lost my job due to my employer's cash flow problem. Finally, I had my epiphany—I had always been at the mercy of a company and its leaders' good or bad decisions. I had never really thought about how I was going to lead my own life, follow my heart, and make a difference in the world. I thought, why can't I be the leader of my life, live from my own authenticity, and serve the right people who are ready and welcome my service?

With the guidance and help of a gracious and successful serial-entrepreneur, I started my first boutique public relations agency. This was also a lifestyle choice, because I now had time to take care of my family and myself. I had the luxury of spending time on self-learning and on my kids' extra-curricular activities. I had the time to cook healthy and nutritious meals, while providing guidance to my kids on life topics that schools do not teach.

I became more balanced and started to commit time to meditation and exercise; most importantly, my family began to learn and grow together. I decided to recharge my batteries and acquire new skills and knowledge. I believed an MBA would prepare me to manage my own business well or allow me to go back to corporate America with a higher position if my business did not work out. Having two young children and a husband who traveled a lot for work, an online MBA was a natural choice. The Jack Welch Management Institute caught my eye during my research, not only because Jack Welch was one of the best CEOs in history but also because its flagship course—Leadership in the 21st Century—was exactly what I was looking for. I was so desperately in search of good leaders to follow and to be a good leader myself, I knew instantly the program was for me.

The MBA study opened my heart and mind, and I now see the world from a different angle. I want to share my learning, so you can plan your future at a young age—or at any age, for that matter. Through this learning, you can minimize failure, and even when failure knocks on the door, you can turn failure into steppingstones to success.

The job, a soon to be outdated relic of the industrial age. The job as we know it is an industrial-age model, and the industrial age is over. A simple search on Google reveals that as high as 80 percent of us don't enjoy—or even hate—our jobs. Very few people work for one employer for two or more decades as was common for the baby boomer generation. A 2016 LinkedIn study of its 500 million users found that millennials—those born between 1980-1996—will change jobs an average of four times in their first 10 years out of college. A Gallup 2016 study of millennials showed that few were committed to their current jobs and that 60 percent were open to new jobs. However, job hoppers often mistakenly believe that they can find more fulfilling work with their next employers. Remember, employers own the jobs, but they do not owe you a career.

This trend will accelerate as automation, robots, artificial intelligence and machine learning continue to improve productivity. In his TED talk *The Real Reason Manufacturing Jobs Are Disappearing*, Augie Picado pointed out that 87 percent of lost manufacturing jobs have been eliminated due to productivity improvement, and those jobs are gone for good. In March 2017, *Fortune* published an article titled *Robots Could Steal 40% of US jobs by 2030* based on a report by consultancy firm PwC. These lost jobs will not be just manufacturing jobs but will include such current jobs as teachers, drivers and accountants—even lawyers and doctors.

Traditionally, the most accepted way to make a living was to work for others by trading talent and time for money and security. And this time is the best time of our days and lives—nine to five, not counting commuting and overtime. However, the good job pool is getting smaller and smaller. Companies are looking for the best talent, but the best talent wants to work for freedom, meaning and self-realization. The new trend is bending toward self-empowered, passion-driven freedom-seekers such as technology entrepreneurs, social entrepreneurs, solo-preneurs, media-preneurs, small business owners, and freelancers.

Futurist and technology media pioneer Kevin Kelly said, "The future happens very slowly and then all at once.... It's going to change everything and affect our infrastructure and businesses in a very dramatic way." Kelly said our society is not prepared for many of these changes, but I want you, the reader of this book, to be prepared.

A new kind of education is needed. Most educational systems around the world use standardized tests to evaluate learning and reward both teachers and students based on test results. This is still "the Factory Model of Education," preparing students to follow the rules and regulations to become productive industrial-age workers. But mainstream schools are not teaching important business skills such as critical and creative thinking, emotional intelligence, problem solving, decision making, interpersonal communication, leadership and change management, while ignoring important life skills such as health, nutrition, personal finance, relationships, mindfulness and seeking happiness from within.

The obsession of parents with a college education is almost psychotic. In the U.S. alone, higher-education costs have increased at twice the rate of inflation, and student debt tops US $1.3 trillion in 2017 and is growing fast. Deep down in our collective subconscious, we believe a college education equals good and lasting jobs. Even though the 2017 report by The Bureau of Labor Statistics reported only a 2.5 percent unemployment rate for college graduates, it is disconcerting to see more and more of today's graduates hopping from job to job, coming back to live with their parents, unable to find a meaningful job. In 1960, the top employers were high-wage companies like GM, AT&T, and GE. Today, the top employers are low-wage companies like Walmart, Yum (Taco Bell, KFC, et al.), and McDonald's. For many college graduates, landing a fulfilling job while paying off their student loans is nearly impossible. Too many have received a degree but not an education.

We need a new kind of education for a fast-changing world. We need talent to solve difficult problems that others have feared to tackle, and leaders who can actually lead. We simply need happy adults who can navigate life's ups and downs without resorting to medication. We need people like Peter Thiel, the successful entrepreneur and venture capitalist who is challenging the current educational status quo. As Thiel sees it, "Today's elite universities are holding back innovation and contributing to a technology deficit that will have disastrous economic consequences. He believes "gumptious" kids (like the ones in his fellowship program) shouldn't spend their late teens and early 20s piling up debt that will push them into gainful but unrewarding jobs. Instead, they should pursue "radical innovation that will benefit society."

We also need a new kind of education to discover and nurture the uniqueness of all our children. According to a quote sometimes attributed to Einstein, "Everybody is a genius. But if you judge a fish by its ability to climb a tree, it will live its whole life believing that it is stupid." The fulfilled and happy people in our society are those who are intrinsically motivated to pursue whole-heartedly their personal passions and live authentically. The TEDx Talk by Adam Leipzig titled *How to Know Your Life Purpose in 5 Minutes* is one of the most viewed presentations on the Internet. Mr. Leipzig reported that 80 percent of his Yale alumni were not happy even after seemingly successful careers of power and wealth. This number matches *Forbes'* data that 81 percent of North American workers are dissatisfied with their work. Leipzig noted the happier 20 percent of his Yale graduates were those "who knew something about their life purpose, because they knew five things: who they were, what they did, who they did it for, what those people wanted or needed, and how they changed as a result." Our current educational system may help you make a living but taking control of your education will help you make a life. Take your education back.

Why MBA before college? I mentioned earlier my "aha moment" from Seth Godin's suggestion that every college student should start a business while in college. I believe learning MBA concepts early will give you the foundation of knowledge and skills to run a business. Successful companies are defined as those that identify, create and deliver products or services that are valued by customers, that make a profit for the owners and investors, while making a positive impact on society. This means that companies need strong leadership and a level of differentiation that distinguishes their products and services in a market dominated by other companies, large or small. It also means that companies need to make meaningful contributions to the communities they serve.

To manage a successful company, you need to learn essential skills that are taught in MBA courses. Knowing these business management principles will give you a better chance to run a successful company. A good MBA program teaches three fundamentals: leadership essentials, business foundations, and entrepreneurship.

Leadership essentials include the areas of what makes a great leader; knowledge and skills of being an effective leader; managing capable people effectively; building a great organizational culture; using business communication skills that share, inspire and persuade; leading change; and living a fulfilled career and personal life.

Business foundations include the areas of strategy, operations management, financial management, and marketing. These are the tools to help you speak the language of business and manage financial resources; understand how to operate the business in the macro-environment outside the business and micro-industry dynamics; deliver high quality products or services efficiently; offer best solutions that solve your customers' pains and problems; and plan your business for long-term success.

Entrepreneurship includes the essential knowledge on how to start a business, how to write a business plan, how to raise money, how to manage the business, and how to plan an exit.

Where to look for business ideas? The media and the public tend to pay attention to technology, software and social media startups, seeing to equate entrepreneurship with media and technology. Elon Musk and Jeff Bezos are the rare models for entrepreneurial success. A wide range of business opportunities that are not primarily driven by technology are available for all of us. By nurturing our curiosity and imagination, observing life and solving interesting problems, we can find great ideas to improve our lives and the lives of others. Just remember, the purpose of a business is to serve the customers and solve customers' problems and pain; in turn both customers and businesses flourish. Through all this, we obtain the opportunity to enrich the lives of our employees, customers and ourselves. Remember, success is just a byproduct when we help enough people solve their biggest and most painful problems.

INSEAD Professors Chan Kim and Renee Mauborgne's bestseller book *Blue Ocean Shift—Beyond Competing: Proven Steps to Inspire Confidence and Seize New Growth* was published in late 2017, and in it the authors coined the word "value innovation." They want businesses to think about creating innovation by asking three questions:

- How does our offering make buyers' lives dramatically more simple, productive, convenient, or fun and stylish?
- How does our offering dramatically reduce buyers' risks? These risks may be financial, physical or emotional (including reputational risk).
- And how does our offering deliver a leap in environmental friendliness, including social consciousness that a buyer values?

An ancient Chinese proverb tells us that "heroes always come out of early youth." Steve Jobs reminded us, "We're all here to put a dent in the Universe. Otherwise why else even be here?" Look at the people who "made a dent in the Universe": J. K. Rolling knew books were her destiny at age five, Larry King knew radio and media were his calling at the same age, Warren Buffet finished reading tax laws in high school, and Bill Gates started tinkering with computers when he was 14 years old. Successful people know. The truth is we all know; we just need to find that small voice deep inside ourselves, that "inner ding" (aptly named by spiritual teacher Louise Hay). When we are in total quietness without noise and thoughts, we can hear that voice and receive that calling. Then we can use the MBA knowledge and tools to implement the idea sparked from our "inner ding." We can build a business, big or small, for-profit or non-profit, and make a dent in the Universe.

References and Suggested Readings

Adkins, A. "Millennials: The Job-Hopping Generation." http://news.gallup.com/businessjournal/191459/millennials-job-hopping-generation.aspx.

Clynes, T. "Peter Thiel Thinks You Should Skip College, and He'll Even Pay You For Your Trouble." http://www.newsweek.com/2017/03/03/peter-thiel-fellowship-college-higher-education-559261.html.

Kim, W. C. and R. Mauborgne. *Blue Ocean Shift: Beyond Competing. Proven Steps to Inspire Confidence and Seize new Growth.* New York, NY: Hachette Books, 2017.

Lacy, S. "Peter Thiel: We're in a Bubble and It's Not the Internet. It's Higher Education." https://techcrunch.com/2011/04/10/peter-thiel-were-in-a-bubble-and-its-not-the-internet-its-higher-education/.

Choi, A. S. "What the Best Education Systems are Doing Right." https://ideas.ted.com/what-the-best-education-systems-are-doing-right/.

CHAPTER 2

LEADERSHIP: INSPIRATION, EDGE AND ADAPTABILITY

"Becoming a leader is synonymous with becoming yourself. It's precisely that simple, and it's also that difficult."
—Warren Bennis, American scholar, author and pioneer in leadership studies

Why Do You Want to Be a Leader?

When I first began sharing what I had learned about leadership with my then 9-year-old daughter Amy, her initial question was, "Why would somebody want to be a leader? Is there a guarantee I won't fail?" I asked her back, "Do you want to become your true self?" "Of course," she replied. "Then becoming a leader starts with being your authentic self, not living a life others expect of you. Isn't that liberating?" "Yes!" she beamed.

Now ask yourself: when you are 80 years old, do you want to spend your time regretting all the things you never tried? Or do you want to have lived a life fueled by your own deepest passion and desire? Do you want to have made a difference in the world with your unique contributions? Do you want to feel a sense of accomplishment? If the answers are yes, then you need to be a leader—lead your own life first, then you'll attract followers.

Leaders come in all shapes and sizes and from entirely different life and career paths. We all know the names of the great leaders who made history: political and military leader George Washington, intellectual leader Socrates, religious leader Mother Teresa, social leader Martin Luther King Jr., economic leader John D. Rockefeller, scientific leader Albert Einstein, artistic leader Leonardo da Vinci, entertainment leader Walt Disney—the list can go on and on. There is a common thread running through all of these exceptional leaders; as *100leaders.org* points out, they were good at being authentic, articulating a vision, motivating others, making effective decisions, confronting tough issues and impacting history.

Not all of us are meant to make the kind of impact these leaders made, but we all need to fulfill a purpose. We need to find that purpose, using it as our compass to lead us from within. We can start by leading our own lives. We can take full responsibility for everything that happens to us. We can start leading in many small ways—a club at school or a community program perhaps.

Young Katherine Commale is a perfect example of early leadership. When she was five years old she learned that malaria kills an African child every 30 seconds. Inspired to save lives, Commale started a nonprofit called *Nothing But Nets*. Her organization has raised over $65 million over the years to help deliver 12 million mosquito bed nets to families in need, along with other crucial malaria interventions like diagnostics, treatment, and training of healthcare workers.

Fortune's "18 Under 18" gives credit to young innovators who are changing the world. These teenagers are running a nanny agency, making commercial drones, selling sports equipment, running an entrepreneurial club, even starting a venture capital firm to support other young entrepreneurs—all before they've even graduated from high school.

What about failure? Does a leader fail? Of course. We all fail at some endeavors, and leaders are no exception. But it all depends how you define failure and success. Abraham Lincoln lost eight elections, failed twice in business, and suffered a nervous breakdown before he became one of the greatest presidents in the history of the U.S. Napoleon Hill, author of *Think and Grow Rich*, stated, "Every failure carries with it a seed of equal or greater opportunity." If you study successful people, you'll see that there is no straight line to success. The reality is more like the long-term stock market chart: a lot of upturns and crevasses, but the general direction is upward. That is the roadmap of our lives, to navigate through those ups and downs towards our highest goal. Of course, you can reduce the chance of failure by acquiring knowledge and skills through reading, from mentors and role models.

Motivational speaker and writer Earl Nightingale said, "Success is the progressive realization of a worthy goal or ideal. People with goals succeed because they know where they're going." When we have a clear intention and goal, when we know our "why," the "how" will come. We will come to see setbacks as learning opportunities, steppingstones to something better and greater.

This book is about encouraging you to start your own passion business while in college. Why? I think college is the perfect time for young people to start a business. It is low risk and high reward. In college, most of you do not have the responsibilities of raising a family and you own little if anything. You can afford to fail because you are still young, and the earlier you test your ideas, the better the chance for success. You also have access to resources such as mentors, your professors and other like-minded students. In addition, your business will give you real world education and leadership skills— much more useful than just academic learning. When you have your own business, you are much more likely to achieve financial prosperity, which means you will have enough money to thrive, to pay your tuition, to live a life on your terms, and to give generously to people and causes you care about.

Life is short. Don't choose to live small and follow in the footsteps of others. In Bronnie Ware's bestselling book, *The Five Regrets of the*

Dying, the number one regret is, "I wish I'd had the courage to live my life the way I knew I should, rather than listening to other people tell me what to do." Do something so the world is better after you leave it. Never wait until it's too late. A business contact of mine worked very hard in his job until he reached his goal—to retire and live happily on his own terms. When he was finally able to retire, he moved to Florida and died of a heart attack within months.

A Leader's Mindset Begins with Purpose

In Terence Mauri's book, *The Leader's Mindset: How to Win in the Age of Disruption,* he stated, "The leader's mindset begins with zero compromise on purpose. It demands that you believe in what you're doing and that your contribution is essential to the world. Those who find their calling and match it with their strengths are happier and more successful."

When we do the work we care about, we can make a great impact on the world. As we have seen, Doreen Virtue painted a beautiful picture of a future in which we will be following our personal aspirations, working together on collective passions and adding meaning to all of our lives. Many people put up with a job they don't like—or even hate—for mostly financial reasons. Some look forward to their retirement as a way to escape from the job they dislike. Monday morning is a drag, and Friday is a blessing. The few lucky ones find their true passion and see working as their source of enjoyment. Warren Buffett tap-dances to work every morning and has no intention of retiring, even at the age of 87; he is doing what he loves every day. His advice? "Find your passion. I was very, very lucky to find it when I was seven or eight years old.... You're lucky in life when you find it. And you can't guarantee you'll find it in your first job out. But I always tell college students that come out, 'Take the job you would take if you were independently wealthy. You're going to do well at it.'"

When I was 18 years old and clueless as to what I wanted to be when I grew up, I followed my parents' path. Both mom and dad chose the most popular career in the 1950s in China—mechanical engineering. Despite the fact that neither of them had fulfilling careers—mom did not like the rigidity of her job, and dad had an impossible employee that made his work and life miserable—both of them told me that engineering would be the easiest way for me to land a job. I studied Biomedical Engineering as my college major for that reason. Although I was good academically, I did not enjoy the learning, nor did I want to practice biomedical engineering. I ended up working in marketing in the healthcare device industry for most of my career, using less than 20 percent of the knowledge I spent five years accumulating. It took me another decade to discover my true passion—finding joy in learning and growing every day, leading change, and sharing my journey with like-minded people. I am still a beginner in the pursuit of a self-actualized life, but I hope my children—and all of you who read this book—will not take the kind of years-long detour I made.

It is never too late to ask the question of your life's purpose. Be mindful and observant of your own thoughts and desires, especially when in silence. Cultivating those desires is a great way to begin. You have the choice to live a life that fulfills your talents and potentials. Abraham Maslow, the leader of the modern positive psychology movement, describes self-actualization as one of the highest human needs that can only be met when you maximize your potential, do the best that you are capable of doing, and make a profound positive difference for the world. How amazing life will be when you fully embody and express who you were meant to become!

Leadership: Principles and Values

Leadership is perhaps one of the most widely discussed and written about subjects in business and politics. Merriam-Webster's data shows that the word "leadership" is in the top one percent of all searches. Amazon offers over 100,000 results when I search for "leadership." Yet leadership is still one of the most difficult qualities to find in people, and we have a serious shortage of strong and capable leaders who can solve our world's mounting problems—a degraded environment, endless wars, and unending poverty.

What is leadership anyway? The dictionary definition of leadership is as a position in a group or organization, as a time when a person holds the position of a leader, and as the power or ability to influence the behavior of other people. Many people confuse leadership with management. They are really two different terms. Managers are those who promote stability, and do things faster, cheaper and more predictably. On the contrary, leaders make something happen, create change and make an impact in our unpredictable world. Effective leaders are characterized as having high emotional intelligence, people who are able to motivate others to achieve strong results, manage conflict, lead change, align teams, and elicit support from the people around them. A leader has the courage to say, "Follow me"—and people do.

There are also the wrong sorts of leadership. We all know leaders who are motivated by immoral reasons, such as power, money, greed, short-term narrow interests, and other ego-driven reasons. On the contrary, great leaders act for moral reasons, such as solving complex problems, being of service to people, and helping others succeed. I believe leadership is to serve more than to take. Leadership is about making others better as a result of your presence and making sure that impact lasts in your absence. Stephen Covey, the author of *Seven Habits of Highly Effective People*, says that "Leadership is more than a position, it is moral authority. Moral authority comes from following universal and timeless principles like honesty, integrity, and treating people with respect."

Although our school system seems to value leadership, there are no classes teaching such leadership skills as emotional intelligence, influencing others, and leading change. We do not need more well-rounded adults who follow instructions, comply with the rules, and follow a career with clear job descriptions. We need more transformative leaders who can tackle the pressing issues of our times, and align with the changes most of us wish to see.

What does a leader do? John Kotter is a Harvard Business School professor and an authority on leadership and change. In his influential *Harvard Business Review* articles and books, he suggests that leaders have these main roles: setting directions, pressing for change, aligning people, and inspiring action. A leader who walks the talk will gain the trust of employees, making them feel safe, willing to innovate, create, take risks, and stretch themselves. John Chambers, the former executive chairman and CEO of Cisco, described his job as having four parts: (1) develop vision and strategy for the company; (2) select, recruit, develop and retain a leadership team to implement the vision and strategy; (3) build a strong and adaptive culture; and (4) communicate in a way that people want to follow the vision.

Are leaders born or made? Although we admire those natural born leaders, leadership can be learned. A set of leadership skills exists that you can learn through training, perception, practice, experience, and failure over time. Even Alexander the Great, one of the greatest military leaders in history and a man who conquered the known world, studied under Aristotle and the best military leaders in the kingdom, including his father.

Leadership principles and values. Jack Welch is the founder of my business school and the legendary CEO of GE who grew the company's value by 4,000 percent during his 20-year tenure. He was hailed as one of the greatest business leaders in the United States. Written with his wife Suzy, his best-selling book *Winning* is the essence of business leadership. The book was written in 2005, but the principles are timeless. Welch's leadership philosophies emphasize growing and helping those you lead. I have summarized his leadership principles below.

1. Leaders relentlessly upgrade their team, using every encounter as an opportunity to evaluate, coach, and build self-confidence.
2. Leaders make sure people not only see the vision, they live and breathe it.
3. Leaders get into everyone's skin, exuding positive energy and optimism.
4. Leaders establish trust with candor, transparency and credit.
5. Leaders have the courage to make unpopular decisions and gut calls.
6. Leaders probe and push with a curiosity that borders on skepticism, making sure their questions are answered with action.
7. Leaders inspire risk taking and learning by setting the example.
8. Leaders celebrate.

The importance of emotional intelligence. The ability to monitor your own and other people's emotions, to distinguish between different emotions and label them appropriately, and to use this information to guide your thinking and behavior together constitute emotional intelligence (EI). According to a 2013 study by American Express, emotional intelligence is one of the biggest predictors of success in the workplace, and a strong driver of leadership and personal excellence.

Daniel Goleman wrote the groundbreaking bestselling book *Emotional Intelligence* in 1995, bringing the EI concept to the world. Goleman identified a group of five skills that enable leaders to maximize their own and their follower's performance. These skills include self-awareness, self-regulation, motivation, empathy, and social skills. Since then, much has been written about emotional intelligence. Here is an overview summary of Goleman's five components of EI, and I suggest you read his book and others on this subject to learn more.

Self-awareness means knowing your emotions, strengths, weaknesses, drives, values and goals, and their impact on others. Highly skilled leaders have self-confidence, realistic self-assessment, and receive constructive criticism openly.

Self-regulation means you can control or redirect disruptive emotions and impulses. By mastering this, you increase your trustworthiness, integrity and comfort with change.

Motivation means you are driven to achieve for the sake of achievement. This connects to finding your life's purpose, because when you have a strong desire to reach your highest goal, you have a passion for work, the courage to face new challenges, the unflagging energy to improve, and optimism in the face of failure. You are less motivated by such ego needs as money and pride.

Empathy means you understand at an emotional level of other's feelings, especially when making decisions. As a result, you are more connected with other people on an emotional level. With empathy, you will have the expertise to attract and retain talent, and the ability to develop others.

Social skills mean you can manage relationships to move people in the desired direction. People with social skills are more persuasive, better at building trust and leading teams, and more effective in leading change.

Our schools still classify kids as gifted solely based on IQ; but research has shown that IQ can only predict 20 percent of future success, while EI contributes as much as 80 percent. However, finding emotional intelligence in the curriculum is sometimes difficult. In order to realize your leadership and entrepreneurial dreams, you can start to strengthen your EI "muscle" through learning, conscious practice and constructive feedback.

Actions! Leadership Starts With You and Within You

Leadership expert John Maxwell says everything in a business rises and falls on leadership. Leadership is a learned skill just like any other. Take actions to beef up your leadership skills and experiences, so that you are well prepared when opportunities show up. The most practical advice is to work on improving yourself first. It is often said that the greatest challenge faced by any leaders is leading themselves.

Be ready and have the desire to lead. Personal leadership is the most important task of any leader, and it starts with accepting responsibilities and a commitment to lead your own life. When you have the desire to contribute to others and make a positive difference in the world, you automatically take the leadership role.

The fastest way to become a leader is to start acting like one. If you are starting off your life, you don't need a title or position to lead; start by leading through influence, leading others in small ways as you gain experience. The world is constantly changing and desperately needs more capable leaders. Show your courage since people follow courage. Be ready and step up and say, "Follow me." A Miami high school student started a program to collect used computers from students and the community. He led a team of students to refurbish the computers and donated them to poor schools in the Caribbean.

Find your purpose and lead from the power within you. Have you noticed that you and your friends tend to have brains that are wired differently, that you are naturally good at some things, while they are good at other things? Observe yourself and seek to understand why this is so. What interesting problems draw your attention like a magnet? What is your unique talent that you can use to serve others? You may discover your unique precious gift and purpose. Successful leaders are often driven by their inner voices and the willingness to do things differently. Find yours.

Good leadership is helping others succeed. Zig Ziglar said, "You get what you want by helping others get what they want." One of the most important aspects of leadership is serving others. Jack Welch emphasizes that, "When you are a leader, it is all about helping others succeed." Leadership isn't about you but about helping others become successful, and about removing the obstacles for the people who follow you.

Strengthen your EI. I have discussed the importance of EI to business and professional success. In essence, your ability to manage your own and other people's emotions is more important to your future success than raw intelligence. Just like leadership, EI can be learned. You can start to understand yourself by taking such self-assessments as the DiSC profile, the Myers-Briggs Type Indicator and the Strong Interest Inventory, which should be available from your high school or college counseling center. When you know your strengths and weaknesses, you can then learn to compensate your weaknesses by selecting the right partners or employees. Empathy, risk taking, overcoming adversity, perseverance, and a positive attitude are great emotional intelligence strengths you can practice and master.

Commit to lifelong learning. All good leaders are lifelong learners. Too many people believe that learning stops with graduation from college. However, the real learning begins after formal education. Highly motivated leaders strive to educate themselves on new concepts and ideas every day. They understand the importance of creating plentiful opportunities in all areas of life. Self-directed learning can involve reading about and analyzing great leaders you admire from history and around the world. Study their behaviors, actions and results. Read a good book every week. Practice meditation and listen to the knowledge and wisdom that already exist within you when you remain quiet. Learn such soft skills as negotiation, communication, and decision-making. Surround yourself with like-minded people or, better yet, people who are smarter than you. In his Stanford commencement speech, Steve Jobs gave this advice: "Stay hungry, stay foolish." Nurture a perpetual hunger for more meaning in your life.

Take actions and practice. Go work for a leader you admire. Find a good mentor in your field that aligns with your goals. Start your own business. Today, opportunities to become an entrepreneur, a social-preneur, a small business owner, or an author have never been more widely available. Find your passion and start your engine. The future is yours. If you must work for others, find a good leader to follow in the area of your passion. If you run into an obstacle, don't stop; work around it, climb over it, or break through it. But never give up.

Seth Godin says, "Leadership is scarce because few people are willing to go through the discomfort required to lead. This scarcity makes leadership valuable." I encourage you to go the extra mile, now and always. As Dr. Wayne Dyer points out, "It is never crowded along the extra mile."

References and Suggested Readings

Goleman, D. *Emotional Intelligence. Why It Can Matter more than IQ.* New York, NY: Bantam Books, 1995.

Mauri, T. *The Leader's Mindset: How to Win in the Age of Disruption.* New York, NY: Morgan James Publishing. 2017.

Marinova, P. "18 Under 18: Meet the Young Innovators Who Are Changing the World." http://fortune.com/2016/09/15/18-entrepreneurs-under-18-teen-business/.

Welch, J. and S. Welch. *Winning.* New York, NY: HarperCollins, 2005.

CHAPTER 3

COMMUNICATION: INFORM, INSPIRE, PERSUADE AND ENGAGE

> "To effectively communicate, we must realize that we are all different in the way we perceive the world and use this understanding as a guide to our communication with others."
> —Tony Robbins, American author, entrepreneur, philanthropist and life coach

Communication skills are one of the most important learnable skills you can possess in dealing with any human relationship. In our daily lives, we constantly communicate our needs, wants, ideas, and feelings with our family and friends. In business, we communicate in a variety of ways. Take these scenarios for example:

- An entrepreneur pitches to potential investors
- An executive negotiates a business deal
- A CEO speaks to employees to raise morale
- A TED Talk speaker inspires the audience with new ideas
- An author writes books or articles to communicate ideas and messages
- A sales person sells a software solution to a customer

- A manager conducts a performance review
- A customer service representative tries to solve a customer problem
- A person goes on an interview for a job
- A company creates an advertising campaign to attract and persuade buyers

All these interactions are intended to inform, inspire, persuade, and engage business stakeholders, including customers, investors, management, and employees. No business can develop or grow without effective communication.

On a professional level, entrepreneurs and employers rank effective business communication as one of the top skills. An effective communicator has the best opportunity to make an outstanding first impression by using powerful words, images and messages to craft strong internal partnerships and develop the foundation of solid business relationships.

Business Communication Strategy

Efficient, appropriate, thoughtful and inspiring messages, and delivery techniques are essential to successful communication. Before you start to communicate either through writing or speaking, you need to think strategically about how you intend to communicate to get the desired response from your audience. You can maximize your results when you understand how to craft messages to the audience's specific needs. In their *Guide to Managerial Communication: Effective Business Writing and Speaking,* Mary Munter and Lynn Hamilton recommend five interconnected variables in any attempt to communicate: (1) communicator strategy, (2) audience strategy, (3) message strategy, (4) channel choice strategy, and (5) culture strategy. Below is a summary of how to use these five strategies.

Communicator strategy. Objectives, style and credibility are the three factors that make up the communicator strategy. All three factors revolve around you, the communicator.

1. **Objectives**. As the communicator, you want to elicit a desired response, action or outcome from your audience. Let's say you have the objective of increasing sales by 20 percent this year. You then define an action objective: add 100 new members to your membership site each month. You subsequently run an affiliate marketing campaign with the objective of having 100 customers sign up for your sales offer.
2. **Style**. According to Munter and Hamilton, a range of communication styles is possible: tell, sell, consult and join. Tell/sell situations include teaching, explaining, persuading or advocating. Use this style when you have sufficient information, want to control the content and do not need to get input from your audience. Use the consult/join style when you want to learn from your audience, involve them, and gain their buy-in. In an ongoing communication of a project, you usually combine these styles. For example, you can use "join" to brainstorm ideas, "consult" to choose one of those ideas, "sell" to persuade your team to adopt that idea, and "tell" to write up the idea once it becomes policy.
3. **Credibility**. Your audience's perceptions of you—their belief, confidence, and faith in you—have a tremendous impact on how you communicate with them. The five credibility factors include: rank (hierarchical power), goodwill (track record and trustworthiness), expertise (knowledge and competence), image (attractiveness, authenticity and sincerity), and common ground (values, ideas, problems or needs). You can enhance your credibility by stressing it before the communication, and earning it after the communication. When you do a great job in communicating, you heighten your credibility.

Audience strategy. Audience strategy means gearing your message toward the audience's needs and interests. This is perhaps the most important aspect of the overall strategy. The more you know about your audience—who they are, what they know, what they feel, what inspires them, what motivates them, and how they can be persuaded—the more effective your communication will be. The more you know about your audience, the better you can target your communication. In certain situations, you need to identify key influencers who can control the outcome of the communication. These influencers can be decision makers, opinion leaders, and gatekeepers who have control over your desired result. Knowing their motivation and concerns will help you prepare better.

The key to persuasion is to emphasize the benefits the audience will get. People always ask, "What's in it for me?" Your communication needs to focus on the tangible benefits (such as profit and result) and other benefits such as a sense of accomplishment, achievement and self-worth. You can also enhance your credibility with these techniques: establish a common ground with your audience, build rapport and a relationship with the audience before the communication, connect with your audience emotionally, stay authentic and communicate with integrity.

Many communicators often overlook the importance of knowing the audience. Learning about your audience can be done by simply asking questions or perhaps by even interviewing several members of your audience. Good questioning and listening can help you understand your audience's problems and motivation.

Message strategy. Crafting a message that connects with your audience is essential. A well-organized message has the following features:

1. Harness the power of the beginning and the ending. The audience has a memory curve and tends to remember the beginning and the ending but not what's in the middle.

Therefore, you can use both the beginning and ending to emphasize your main ideas and conclusions prominently.
2. Overcome the retention dip in the middle. You can chunk content into smaller sections to increase audience retention. In order to avoid data dump, you need to limit your main points to no more than five. Some useful techniques are: repetition, flagging signals such as "if you only remember one thing," using unexpected and dramatic changes and providing visual aids such as a striking image or video.
3. Organize your message. You can organize your informative message (tell) around key points, key questions, processes or steps, and comparisons. You can organize your persuasive communication (sell) around a list of recommendations or a list of benefits, problems, and possible solutions.
4. Connect through stories. We all remember some unforgettable stories because stories provide a powerful way to connect and learn. A good communicator has to learn to tell good stories. According to Donald Miller, the author and owner of *Story Brand*, a story is like a hidden language every human understands. Stories make the abstract real and meaningful, increase stickiness, engage audiences and build relationships, sell products or services, and build organizational spirit. You need to choose stories wisely by using them at the right time, making a point, and invoking classic themes. According to Munter and Hamilton, a well-structured story has seven elements: (1) An inciting incident to launch the story; (2) A protagonist, a main character that your audience wants to see succeed; (3) obstacles and conflicts; (4) something significant at stake, which could be money, reputation, relationship or even lives; (5) a point of choice or decision, a moment that the protagonist must decide and act; (6) a result that leads to a clear outcome; and (7) concrete details to help the audience visualize what happened.

In summary, a clear message structure uses a powerful opening and closing to emphasize audience benefits; uses a strong middle structure that is organized around problem/solution, contrast between options, or pros/cons; and works stories into the communication.

Channel choice strategy. Channel (aka medium) is how you send your message to your audience. Communication must be tailored and crafted differently for different media, making it both a challenge and an opportunity for communicators. In the digital age, we have many media to choose from, including an abundance of social media platforms and the availability of low cost personal broadcasting channels. In fact, many new entrepreneurs are media-preneurs, who build business and personal brands online. They can be coaches, speakers, authors, expert-turned-teachers, and Internet marketers. Many of these media-preneurs have built multi-million dollar businesses through blogs, podcasts, vlogs, personal YouTube channels, webinars and online courses by focusing on their passions.

Although channel choices are abundant, they still fall into two categories: written and spoken. In the written form, we have print copy, email, website, blog, book, text message, tweet and other social media. In the spoken form, we have speaking at live events, presentations, podcasts, face-to-face, phone, conference call, video, video call, video streaming/broadcasting (such as YouTube Live and Facebook Live), webinar and many more.

Over the past decade, social media has taken the world by storm: Facebook, Twitter, LinkedIn, Instagram, Snapchat, Pinterest, WeChat—the list goes on and on. Social media shortens distances and makes daily broadcasting and messaging instant and super easy. Email is a great channel to reach your audience easily and cost-effectively, and text messaging has largely replaced phone calls. Podcasts have become the new radio show, and YouTube has become your personal TV channel, reaching anyone from anywhere in the world asynchronously.

In the business world, a good communicator uses a combined

channel strategy. For example, you can hold a series of one-on-one meetings to build rapport and a relationship with influencers, make a presentation to a bigger audience to build community, and share educational videos, blogs or emails with your audience to aid their decision making.

When choosing channels, you must consider your objective, audience, and message thoughtfully. The issues you should consider include: the audience and culture preference, interaction level, verbal or non-verbal, needs of permanent record, control of timing, level of details and risks. The preference needs to come from your audience, not from your own comfort level.

Great communication can help build and expand a business. Gary Keller, the founder of Keller William Realty, is a prime example. Keller dedicated himself to book writing and made it his mission to change the way people think about the real estate business. Keller and his two co-authors Dave Jenks and Jay Papasan have written books with millions of copies sold and won many awards over nearly two decades. This business strategy propelled Keller Williams to become one of the world's largest real estate franchises.

Culture strategy. The world is becoming more and more interconnected. Cultural norms, which mean most people in a group behave in certain ways most of the time, is valuable to communicators. The audience's attitudes toward time, fate, credibility, communication style, audience selection, persuasion, gender, message structure, channel choice, nonverbal behavior, greetings and hospitalities are all important factors to consider when preparing your communication.

The Importance of Language and Communication Skills

There are several important language and communication skills you need to master through ongoing practice: speaking, writing, negotiating, listening, reading, selling, and networking. These skills are interconnected to a certain degree. Proficiency in all these areas will help you stand out from the rest.

Speaking. In day-to-day business, this involves speaking to an audience, giving presentations, hosting Q&A sessions, facilitating and participating in meetings, doing media interviews, taping a video or giving online presentations. Although different situations require different verbal structures, all speaking communication involves planning ahead. Typical planning includes analyzing your audience, using effective openings and closings, planning your main points and stories, thinking about questions and planning your responses in advance. Experienced speakers emphasize advance testing when using technologies, knowing when you are scheduled to speak, and learning about the location ambience and layout, so you are fully prepared.

Among all the various speaking situations, giving a speech is the most effective way to communicate to an audience. Great speakers have the ability to put words together in a meaningful and inspirational way to reflect opinions, thoughts and feelings. Strong speaking skills can enhance your career as employers in general value the ability to speak well. In addition to being a powerful way to convey messages and thoughts, strong verbal skills increase your negotiation skills, improve credibility, and self-confidence. A good speaker is usually a good storyteller and uses data, stories and examples to influence and connect with the audience for a desired outcome.

Although many people are afraid of public speaking or have problems delivering their thoughts through speeches in a believable way, speaking is a skill that can be learned and developed. Develop and hone your speaking skills through practice and constant application. Hard work always pays off. You can watch TED talks to learn how master speakers present their ideas. You can join a debate club at your school or join Toastmasters or Ted-Ed clubs for youth, which are educational organizations to help members improve communication, public speaking, and leadership skills.

Many tactics and insights can be used to overcome the fear of public speaking. You can visualize the steps to deliver a successful speech. You can focus on the valuable information the audience can use from your communication. This helps you face and accept your fear and still have the courage to speak. The other useful advice is to be who you are and communicate authentically. When you speak from passion, expertise and a strong inner desire to share your ideas, all the fears of speaking become manageable. Your presence shines through and your authenticity creates trust and builds credibility. Sometimes fear is there to remind you that you have not fully prepared, so get more practice and develop a deep understanding of your topic. We tend to be our own worst critics, but we can transform that negative energy into a supportive and encouraging one. We can give ourselves credit for rising to our best effort and assure that we are getting better and better with each experience.

Writing. Good writing shows a mastery of language. We all need good writing skills to properly convey our ideas and concepts. We spend a lot of time writing in both academic and business settings. We write compositions, book reports and essays at school, and then write emails, memos, plans and proposals in business.

While both academic writing and business writing require well thought out ideas and clear and precise communication, the two are quite different. Business writing should be brief, informative and to the point. Your purpose is to help your audience (colleague, boss, investors and customers) get the important points with clarity. In addition to words, you can make your case solid by using financial numbers, data, graphs and examples. You also adapt your style to different situations. For example, if you write social media posts for business, you can use a friendly, conversational and casual tone to engage viewers.

An effective writing process usually starts with setting a clear strategy, especially with the audience's needs and expectations in mind. Then the actual process involves researching, organizing, drafting, revising, and editing. Like anything in life, practice makes perfect, and writing is no exception. As an engineering student, I dreaded writing. When I started my MBA program, I had concerns about writing essays and papers. But after three years of focused writing and reading, I started to embrace and even love writing. I even began to write a journal every day to jot down my new learnings, thoughts, ideas, challenges and reflections. Writing sparks creativity and inspired me to write this book.

Maybe I am old school, but I want to emphasize the importance of proper spelling and grammar. Younger generations growing up in the digital age have become accustomed to casual communication, especially in social media. In the business world, however, proper grammar and spelling—instead of modern abbreviations—are always required. You can learn to write well by reading books such as *On Writing Well* and learn from online resources such as the Perdue Online Writing Lab, a place with numerous writing resources and instructional materials.

Negotiation. The definition of negotiation refers to a discussion aimed at reaching an agreement. In business, negotiation for a win-win outcome is a skill that is more difficult to master than many other skills. It involves emotional intelligence such as empathy, influence, patience and listening. Whether we realize it or not, we spend a lot of time negotiating with business partners, bosses, employees, suppliers, sellers, landlord, car dealers, bankers, and even our loved ones. We find ourselves negotiating a salary and raises, buying a home, leasing a car, renegotiating rent, and deliberating with our partner.

In business, negotiation is an integral part of creating value for the organization, whether you are seeking funding or resources for your business, deciding on a new hire's salary, or inking a high-stakes deal for your company. Learning effective business negotiation skills helps you achieve better results in both formal and informational negotiations, build your confidence and create positive relationships with all parties.

Many workshops, seminars, online courses and books teach

negotiation skills, strategies, tactics and techniques. Business schools such as Harvard and Wharton offer courses on negotiation. Coursera and other online learning platforms have online courses too. Gary Karrass is an internationally recognized authority on negotiation. His company has trained over one million people in negotiation. His book, *Negotiate to Close: How to Make More Successful Deals*, shares the skills and techniques to make better business deals. Christopher Voss, an expert in high-stakes negotiations, is a former international hostage negotiator for the FBI. His book, *Never Split the Difference: Negotiating as if Your Life Depended on It*, shares remarkable insights, principles and strategies on negotiation. Below is a brief summary of the negotiation process: preparation, the actual negotiation, closure, and analysis of lessons learned.

The preparation process. Negotiation starts before the actual meeting. Good planning of the negotiation strategy you intend to use is one of the most important steps you can take. You can maximize opportunity through planning in the following areas:

- Establish your goals and objectives
- Evaluate your own skills
- Gather information and the other party's interests, priorities and positions
- Know the people involved and how personal biases and cultural differences impact negotiation
- Build a rapport with the other party if possible
- Determine your best alternative to a negotiated agreement, which means what is your best option if you cannot reach an agreement with the other party.

Setting your goals is the first and most important question to ask before going into a negotiation. You need to define your primary goal or a measurement of success before the negotiation starts. In most business situations, the goal should be to reach an agreement that both parties feel good about. Sometimes this involves creating an "enlarged pie," inventing options for mutual gains, and transforming competition into cooperation.

The negotiation process. Many tactics can be used in the negotiation itself. The opening phase sets the tone for the rest of the negotiation. You should spend some time building rapport and making sure the other party feels at ease and comfortable. While convincing and persuading are the main goals during negotiation, you need the powerful emotional intelligence skills listed below:

- Concentration and patience
- Separate people from the issues, especially when dealing with irrational people and challenging relationships
- Active listening and asking questions to clarify any ambiguous points
- Paying attention to body language
- Making offers at the right time and in the right way
- Transforming competition into cooperation and opponents into partners
- Recognizing when to walk away from the table

Closure. Although sealing an agreement that both parties feel is fair or win/win with a written document is the ultimate goal, it is equally important to do a post-negotiation review. This is the time when you review each element and find out what went well and what needs to be improved. This valuable process can teach you lessons on how to negotiate better in the future.

Active listening. Listening is crucial in business communication, especially in negotiating, facilitating meetings, gathering feedback, and conducting Q&A sessions. Active listening helps you understand your audience, and in turn, you can resonate, serve and delight your audience when communicating. There is a saying goes that "God gave us two ears and one mouth, so we ought to listen twice as much as we speak." To listen actively involves skillful pauses during speaking, repeating the other's words, and asking questions.

Reading. Reading is the foundation of good writing, and even leadership skills. Harry S. Truman said, "Not all readers are leaders, but all leaders are readers." The authors usually put a lot of effort, experience, and wisdom into their books. Through books, you gain valuable knowledge and indirect experience that elevates you. When you read a good book, it is almost like having one-on-one time with a smart person, an incredible experience to enrich your own life. Reading also improves writing. Du Fu, a famous Chinese poet who lived 1,300 years ago said, "Having read ten thousand volumes of books, I wrote as if I were led by God." When you read widely, you will wisely write.

Selling skills. Jeff Haden wrote an article in the *Inc.* magazine after interviewing 20 business owners and CEOs, who all believed selling skills contributed the most to their success. Selling is a form of communication. Selling skills extend beyond the jobs of the sales department. When you persuade stakeholders such as investors, customers, suppliers or employees to make a decision to invest, buy or work with you, you are selling and convincing them. Good selling is explaining the logic and benefit of a decision while building trust, not manipulating or pressuring as you might find in a cold call or the stereotyped used car sales experience. Candor and integrity go a long way in selling. We are all customers at some point in life, and we know customers like to buy, not to be sold. Sell the way the customer wants to buy.

David Schwedel, an experienced entrepreneur and investor, once advised a new college student to sharpen his selling skills before getting into finance: "The best sales training is to work in an organization where you are passionate about the product or service the company offers. If you are knowledgeable and passionate about what you are doing, you will establish your credibility and gain a person's respect and trust, you will never have to sell anything to anyone."

Networking skills. Networking is building and maintaining contacts and relationships with other people. The saying "It's not what you know, but who you know" is true in business. To operate a business, you need to connect with like-minded people whom you can work with or improve you in some way. The knowledge and connection to a community pays dividends. Some even go further to suggest that your net worth is only as good as your network. A good business network can also be a safety net, and means you have more people to rely on when you require help, advice, information or services.

Networking is time consuming, so quality trumps quantity. Effective networking involves picking the right event and the right people. Always find the person who is motivated, interesting and ambitious, and aim to build a long-lasting relationship. To start a relationship, you can discover a way to help the person you want to connect with. A generous spirit and a genuinely helpful attitude will attract people to you. You may also want to network with important people in your niche. You can learn what makes them successful, sparking new creative ideas for yourself.

Mastermind group. What is called a Mastermind Group is a higher form business networking. A mastermind group consists of people who meet regularly to discuss important personal or business issues in an honest and compassionate environment. The group uses brainstorming, education, feedback, and peer-to-peer accountability and support in order to grow each other's business, implement best practices, and adopt positive personal habits and behaviors. Napoleon Hill wrote about mastermind groups in his famous book *Think and Grow Rich,* which was first published in 1937, yet remains popular to this day. Hill said, "No mind is complete by itself. It needs contact and association with other minds to grow and expand." He credited mastermind groups as the cornerstone to all great achievements.

In summary, every day and in every way, we are communicating through words, actions and thoughts. Great political and business leaders are remembered by their power to communicate effectively. Even today's technology leaders are required to communicate clearly on their big ideas in order to innovate and collaborate. We need our ideas and efforts to resonate with our audiences. We must take communication skills seriously and create a plan to continuously improve these skills.

References and Suggested Readings

Hill, N. *Think and Grow Rich!* The Original, An Official Publication of The Napoleon Hill Foundation. 1937, 2016.

Karrass, G. *Negotiate to Close: How to Make More Successful Deals.* New York, NY: Simon & Schuster, Inc., 1985.

Munter, M. and L. Hamilton, L. *Guide to Managerial Communication. Effective Business Writing and Speaking.* 2nd ed. London: Pearson Education, 2014.

Purdue Online Writing Lab. https://owl.purdue.edu/owl/purdue_owl.html

Satell, G. "Why Communication is Today's Most Important Skill." https://www.forbes.com/sites/gregsatell/2015/02/06/why-communication-is-todays-most-important-skill/#2e9f8081100b

Voss, C. and T. Raz. *Never Split the Difference: Negotiating as if Your Life Depended on.* New York, NY: HarperCollins, 2016.

CHAPTER 4

PEOPLE MANAGEMENT: THE RIGHT PEOPLE FOR YOUR SUCCESS

> "Great companies don't hire skilled people and motivate them, they hire already motivated people and inspire them."
>
> —Simon Sinek, British-American author, motivational speaker and marketing consultant

To my 12-year-old son Ian, the topic of people management brings up two images in his mind—Bill Gates and Paul Allen starting Microsoft, and a boss firing an employee who messed up at work. It is quite true that people management begins with partnering and hiring, and sometimes ends up with the unfortunate event of letting go of a bad hire. Of course, there are the incentivizing, developing, and retaining talented people in between.

Companies are not just services, products or technologies, they are first and foremost people. You cannot build a lasting company without great people. The quality of the leader is reflected by the quality of the people. Winning leaders always surround themselves with great people, people that are better than they are. On a more practical level, learning people management principles can be applied to your life to help you find, develop, retain and let go of friends.

Jim Rohn says, "You are the average of the five people you spend the most time with." The people around you profoundly affect your personal success.

People management is different than what most human resources (HR) departments are doing in a typical company. When Jack Welch was the CEO of GE, he made a point that HR had power equal to the Chief Financial Officer (CFO) of the company. He has an enormous love of people, and saw the HR function as the engine to build "A-level" talents. He advocated filling HR with special people "who are part pastor (hearing all sins and complaints without recrimination), and part parent (loving and nurturing, but giving it to you straight when you're off track)." As a future leader and business owner, it is important for you to learn, practice and master the art and science of people management. In the early stage of your company, you are most likely to be that pastor/parent HR person who hires, nurtures, and develops talents.

Why is People Management So Important?

Brian Tracy says, "Leaders know that the greatest limitation in any endeavor is talented people." High-achievers can have an enormous impact on business results. Most businesses fail because of people-related reasons—failure in the leadership, hiring the wrong people, or failing to adapt to change. That is why Jim Collins in his all-time bestselling business book *Good to Great* concluded:

> The good-to-great leaders began the transformation by first getting the right people on the bus (and the wrong people off the bus), and then figured out where to drive it. The key point is that "who" questions come before "what" decisions—before vision, before strategy, before organization

structure, before tactics (to-do). First who, then what, as a rigorous discipline, consistently applied.

It does not matter if you run your own small business, or if you plan to grow your startup into the next Google or Facebook, people management should be your top priority, especially when you build your first team, and hire senior leaders. Good venture capital firms always look at the leadership team before business ideas when making an investment decision. An A-team with a B-level idea is always better than a B-team implementing an A-idea.

However, great people decisions are really hard. As Jack Welch said, "Hiring good people is hard, hiring great people is brutally hard." In his book *Great People Decisions,* executive recruiting expert Claudio Fernandez Aroaz concluded that hiring managers fall into one of four common traps: statistical odds, difficulty in assessing candidates, psychological biases, and the wrong incentives from both the candidate and the hiring company.

Over-confidence in human nature tends to drive managers to hire quickly, but the odds are against them. According to Aroaz's calculation, even with the intention of hiring the top 10 percent of candidates with 90 percent accuracy, managers are still likely to be wrong half the time. Read the book *Great People Decisions* to understand his calculations and conclusions. Jack Welch, who famously developed great CEOs for many Fortune 100 companies, humbly claimed he only got 80 percent right throughout his career. Many intangible competencies such as perseverance, curiosity, and an optimistic attitude are rarely found on a resume, and are even harder to assess during an interview. Human psychology biases and emotional traps also work against us; these biases include procrastination, choosing people who are like you or you like, herding mentality, making judgment, saving face to cover our mistakes, and many more.

Hiring is expensive, and a poorly managed selection and interview process is costly. A bad hire will add much more cost to your company than the person's salary. An *Inc.* magazine article showed that the real cost of onboarding is about $240,000 for each senior-level leader. A 2013 CareerBuilder survey showed a single bad hire for just an average position could cost more than $50,000. Tangible and intangible losses include the loss of productivity; reduced employee morale; and the additional expenses to screen, interview, hire, and train a replacement. Worse, a bad hire in certain key positions can drive your loyal customers away. In addition, you cannot overlook the effects on the so-called "bad hire"—another human being with self-esteem, life, family, and emotional involvement.

Good people decisions can even save you in your personal life. I want to retell an amazing story, although I can't locate the source. A high school boy wanted to borrow his parents' car to go to "the party of the year" in his town on a Saturday night. But both of his parents had commitments and could not lend him their cars. The boy decided to stay at home. When the curious father questioned the boy why he did not ask for a ride with his friend who had a car, the boy said he had seen his friend "drink and drive" and did not want to take the risk. That night, the boy's friend drove himself and several other kids into a valley and died. Yes, knowing your friend could save your life.

How to Hire Great People

Hiring the right people is the first key step for management excellence. Your business success is highly dependent on getting the right people in the right place. The principle of "hiring hard and managing easy" should be your guide. One suggestion is never hire to fill a position quickly because you are overwhelmed with work. Take your time in the hiring process and select carefully.

It is always great to learn from successful leaders about how to find great people. With his decades of experience hiring and grooming CEO-level leaders, Jack Welch outlined three concepts to identify competent people: (1) the three acid tests, (2) the 4-E plus 1-P framework, and (3) the four top leadership characteristics—three brilliant insights into how to find high-quality people. These insights are summarized below, and you can learn more in his book *Winning*.

1. **The three acid tests:** integrity, intelligence, and maturity. The acid tests are strong indicators of whether a person has the most basic qualities of a well-functioning human being.

Integrity. Oprah Winfrey says it best: "Real integrity is doing the right thing, knowing that nobody's going to know whether you did it or not." People with integrity don't cheat, and they do the right thing simply because it is the right thing to do. They tell the truth, keep promises, are ethical, take responsibilities and own their mistakes. They tell the truth even when the truth is ugly. You can trust people with integrity.

Integrity is the quality that supports all other qualities. There are no moral shortcuts in both life and business. Leadership integrity supports a candor-based culture, as the leaders are secure enough to be surrounded by people who tell the truth—instead of yes-people who say what they want to hear.

Intelligence. IQ, EI, and educational background can be good indicators of intelligence but should not be taken individually. According to Jack Welch, a strong dose of intellectual curiosity along with a breadth of knowledge to lead other smart people is mandatory in today's complex world.

Maturity. In psychology, maturity means the ability to respond to the environment in an appropriate manner. Jack Welch famously said, "People can be mature at any age, and immature too." Maturity is part of emotional intelligence, since mature people can handle both adversity and achievement. They know that hurdles and setbacks in life are not destiny but instead chances to learn.

2. **The 4E plus 1P Framework:** Energy, Energize, Edge,

Execute, and Passion. The first of the four E's stands for positive energy. People with positive energy love life, are optimistic, and thrive on action. The second E is the ability to energize, arouse and inspire others. The third E is edge, which is the courage to make tough decisions even without complete information or when facing a dilemma. The fourth E is execute, the ability to put decisions into action, and get the job done in spite of obstacles. People who can execute get the desired results. P is for passion. Jack Welch says that people with passion have "the juice for life in their veins."

Many successful companies and entrepreneurs believe that they should hire people for their attitude rather than experience. The idea is you can train and teach skills, but you cannot teach attitude. Southwest Airlines has been known to manage its human capital as a core strategy and competitive advantage. The airline hires people with the perfect blend of positive energy, self-confidence, humor, genuineness, and team spirit to match its fun and customer-obsessed culture.

3. ***Additional qualities for leadership roles:*** According to Jack Welch, leadership positions require additional qualities—authenticity, foreseeing changes, surrounding themselves with people better and smarter than them, and heavy-duty resilience.

Authenticity means being your true self and knowing what you stand for, especially when faced with hard decisions and unpopular positions. People who have self-confidence and self-esteem accept themselves and live authentically in both their business and personal lives.

Foreseeing change characterizes leaders who have a sixth sense, and the ability to predict forces and events that would drastically interrupt their business and market so that they can take actions before it is too late.

Surrounding people better than the leader reflects the courage and self-confidence leaders have. Strong leaders dare to be the "dumbest" person in the room, because it opens their eyes to new and bigger ideas. They are willing to embrace diversity, candor, disagreement, and challenging ideas in order to make the best decisions.

Resilience means that a leader can learn from mistakes and reengage with conviction and confidence. We all have made mistakes, hit roadblocks and fell. In Angela Duckworth's best-selling book *Grit*, she defined "grit" as the ability to sustain interest and effort towards long-term goals. It is linked with self-control and deferring short term gratification. In the leadership chapter, we talked about having a burning desire and a strong life purpose—a great foundation for heavy-duty resilience. As Henry David Thoreau says, "If one advances confidently in the direction of his dreams, and endeavors to live the life which he imagined, he will meet with a success unexpected in common hours."

4. ***Lifelong learner:*** I am adding this quality because of its importance in our fast-changing world. Successful leaders are motivated and committed to developing their skills through lifelong learning. Speaker, author and consultant Matthew Kelly encourages people to grow a little bit every day in four areas—physical, emotional, intellectual and spiritual. The compound growth will be phenomenal, since one percent of growth every day equals 38 times of growth in a year. When both your company culture and employees have an eagerness to grow and learn, you are building a winning business.

Take reference checks seriously. Reference checking is a must-do step before making a hiring decision. Although a job candidate always submits contact names for reference, do not let the candidate dictate whom you speak to. Plan your own reference check carefully to include the candidate's previous managers, peers and direct reports if the candidate supervised others. For people who have been working in an industry for a while, you can check reputations through someone who knows the candidates well. When calling the reference, you should always ask open ended questions to verify the reference's relationship with the candidate, discuss the job title, duties and work performance, attitude, personality, work ethic, strengths and weaknesses, and reason for leaving. At the end of the conversation, ask two questions: "If you could, would you re-hire this person?" and "Is there anything else I should know about this person?" Drill down if there are any potential concerns. Remember, you cannot change people, so find the ones that already align with your goals and culture.

How to Retain Talented People

Jack Welch likes to compare business with sports: "The team that puts the best people on the field and gets them playing together wins. It is that simple." Forming people into a winning team is both an art and a science.

Once you have hired the best people, it is now up to you to get them working together as a winning team. You need an effective system to motivate and retain talent, since good people always look for growth opportunities, and jobs that are well suited to their talents and interests. Your talent-retaining strategy involves inspiring jobs, money, recognition, and training—a system that aligns with the employee's goals.

Sharing the common goal with your employees. Abraham Maslow, the American psychologist who is best known for his Hierarchy of Needs, developed a pyramid showing people's evolving needs. People start with a desire for basic physiological needs: air, food, clothing, and shelter, which form the bottom of the pyramid. Once these basic needs are met, people seek such safety and social needs as love and belongingness. Then people move up to esteem needs, and eventually to self-actualization and self-transcendence needs. Self-actualization and self-transcendence are the highest levels, which mean to realize one's personal potential, personal growth, self-fulfillment, peak experiences, and serving something greater than oneself.

Most talented workers are striving to reach the top of Maslow's pyramid, so the work they do must provide meaning and fulfillment. In a top-viewed TED talk by Simon Sinek, *How Great Leaders Inspire Action*, he eloquently said, "successful people or organizations know why they do what they do, which means 'What's your purpose? What's your cause? What's your belief? Why does your organization exist? Why do you get out of bed in the morning? And why should anyone care?'" You need to have good answers to these questions, so you can rally your talented workers. You need to make sure your people share your goals and beliefs, and feel they are playing an important role in achieving those goals and worthy ideals. This requires you to communicate how an employee's job matters, so he or she is committed to it. Frequent and transparent communications make a huge difference. Don't treat your people like mushrooms by keeping them in the dark and feeding them manure.

Develop a meaningful evaluation system. Your company needs to have a clear and simple evaluation system, which contains relevant, agreed-upon criteria that relate directly to the employee's performance. Jack Welch always evaluated his direct reports on handwritten notes with two columns: what he thought the person did well, and how he thought the person could improve. He did this frequently, finding every meeting a chance to observe, coach and develop people.

Offer personal development and growth. Jack Welch stated, "When you become a leader, it is all about them [the people you lead]." Great leaders are intensely people-driven, and they constantly focus on developing and upgrading the skills of their people. In a well-managed company, employees know their career paths and leadership development opportunities, so they know that when the company grows, they will also have a successful career. Good internal and external training and development programs also empower employees. Training motivates people by showing them a way to grow, that the company cares, and that they have a future with the company.

Form a great culture. An organizational culture that encourages lifelong learning, adapting to changes, and engaging the world with an open and curious mind will keep inspired employees. In addition, stimulating work, recognition, celebration, and flexible working hours are great incentives for star employees. Good leaders design their organizations as flat as possible, with clear responsibilities and reporting relationships. In a new startup where money can be limited, you can give your people three things to make them happy—your attention, your affection, and your appreciation. Those free little things can go a long way.

Be a leader people want to follow. People love following leaders who have high emotional intelligence, and who focus on connecting, relating and emotionally engaging with employees in the pursuit of a meaningful and purposeful mission. Leadership guru John Maxwell says, "There are five nonnegotiable characteristics that every effective leader must have: a sense of calling, an ability to communicate, creativity in problem solving, generosity, and consistency." Always ask yourself the question every morning, "How can I continue to grow myself into a more effective leader?"

How to Fire People

Although you may have the best hiring process, the chance is still there that you may hire the wrong person. One of the sad parts of being in business is needing to let people go. It is hard for both you and the person being asked to leave. It is never as simple as Donald Trump's "You are fired" in *The Apprentice* reality show.

When is the appropriate time to fire somebody? According to leadership guru Brian Tracy, the answer is the first time it crosses your mind. He points out the longer you wait, the more you look like an incompetent leader who rewards incompetence and poor behavior. If a partner or an employee does not fit in your culture, lacks the capabilities to perform, or does not behave ethically, it is your job to let that person go. If you drag it on because that person is your friend, or a high achiever in a few areas, you will demoralize your entire company and team by keeping that person. You are indirectly saying that what that person has been doing is encouraged in the company. In addition, sometimes today's high performers do not always live up to their future potential, so there will be times that you will need new blood who can scale and grow with your business. There are three scenarios when you need to let people go:

- Integrity violations. This situation must be dealt with immediately and without hesitation. The organization should know the "why", so no future breaches of rules and ethics are tolerated.
- Layoff due to the economy. The economy and industry go through cycles, and good leaders keep their employees informed through frequent communication, so that employees know the state of the business. Employees should not be surprised by layoffs.
- Firing for nonperformance. This is the most delicate situation, because too many companies set vague performance measures. You need to document performance expectations, and during evaluations state clearly if an employee is missing the mark. The employee should not really be surprised when the firing comes.

Jack Welch suggests that managers fully own the firing process, guided by two principles: no surprise and minimal humiliation. You need to fire with respect. It is too late to use the final meeting to correct an attitude and improve the person. According to Gavin de Becker, author of *The Gift of Fear*, instead of justifying or convincing the employee, the wiser course is to "describe the decision in general terms, saying it is best for both parties. Explain that employment is a two-way street and the present situation isn't serving either way. Recognize the employee is a capable person but this job does not provide the best environment for the person to excel in."

De Backer suggests a firing should take place at the end of the day, and at the end of the week, so the person has some time and space to ride out the high emotion. To the person who is let go, being fired can be a big ego killer. If you have the resources, you can offer them a generous package, or perhaps gift them with a course or books so they can deal with their situation and move on.

In addition, every person who leaves is going to represent your company and can either bad mouth or praise the company. One CEO recounted a time when his company did a poor job of letting a senior employee go. The former employee went on to join one of the company's customers. The first thing the disgruntled ex-employee did was cancel a contract with his former company, a contract worth a couple of million dollars. The improper termination cost the company greatly.

In summary, here are some main points to help you succeed in people management:

1. Learn the science and art of hiring. Learn from the masters by reading books such as *Great People Decisions* and *Winning*, and learn from mentors and other successful leaders.
2. Never rush to hire someone who can "hit the ground running." Take your time to write down job and attitude requirements, develop your interview process following the framework discussed above, learn the art of observing people, and acquire skills on how to effectively hire the right people.
3. Find and interview the first 12 to 20 people and build a benchmark of quality you are looking for, and then hire the next candidate who meets all your criteria.

4. Do not hire solely on experience and skills; hire on emotional intelligence, behavior and attitude. Hire employees who can grow with the company, instead of filling a role.

References and Suggested Readings

Araoz, C.F. *Great People Decisions*. Hoboken, NJ: John Wiley & Sons, 2007.
Collins, J. *Good to Great*. New York, NY: HarperCollins, 2001.
De Becker, G. *The Gift of Fear*. New York, NY: Dell Publishing, 1997.
Duckworth, A. *Grit: The Power of Passion and Perseverance*. New York, NY: Simon & Schuster, Inc., 2016.
Martin, J. and C. Schmidt. "How to Keep your Top Talent." *Harvard Business Review*. May 2010.
Tracy, B. "Brian Tracy on How to Hire the Right People." *American Management Association*. http://www.amanet.org/training/articles/Brian-Tracy-on-How-to-Hire-the-Right-People.aspx.
Welch, J. and S. Welch. *Winning*. New York, NY: HarperCollins, 2005.

CHAPTER 5

FINANCIAL MANAGEMENT: LEARN THE LANGUAGE OF BUSINESS

"You have to understand accounting and you have to understand the nuances of accounting. It's the language of business and it's an imperfect language, but unless you are willing to put in the effort to learn accounting—how to read and interpret financial statements—you really shouldn't select stocks yourself."

—Warren Buffett, American business magnate, investor, and philanthropist

Accounting is the "language of business," and finance is "the artery leading straight to the heart of every business"; both analogies illustrate the importance of finance and accounting in business. Although in the above quote, Warren Buffett refers to the importance of accounting to stock selection, accounting is equally important to run a successful company, since it needs to have sufficient capital to carry out business plans and support daily operations. A business owner must have both financial integrity and a degree of financial competence. Financial management is where you learn to speak with numbers, develop fluency in financial concepts, principles and tools, and maximize the impact of your financial decisions.

What is the difference between accounting and finance? Accounting is the system of recording and summarizing financial transactions; and analyzing, verifying and reporting the results. Accounting also includes the guidelines, principles and procedures of an accounting system. Finance is the art and science of planning and distributing a business's assets. Typical corporate finance involves reading, understanding and analyzing financial data, and applying managerial accounting concepts such as costing, variance analysis, forecasting, and capital budgeting.

Because of the difference between accounting and finance, a company usually has two distinct positions: accounting (recording and reporting all financial transactions) and finance (managing the company's financial resources). While the two roles can be combined for a small business, the financial department has the following key responsibilities:

1. Facilitate operations and manage money in and money out, which include cash collections from customers (accounts receivable), paying suppliers (accounts payable), purchasing, inventory control and payroll.
2. Prepare financial reports per generally accepted accounting principles (GAAP) for audit. The typical reports include but are not limited to balance sheets, income statements and cash flow statements.
3. File tax returns on federal and state income taxes, sales tax, payroll tax, and foreign tax if applicable.
4. Perform managerial accounting to identify, measure, analyze, interpret, and communicate financial information for decision making in the pursuit of the organization's goals.

This chapter provides an overview of basic accounting and finance concepts. It does not replace the need to consult or hire an accountant or CPA when you start a business. You can also acquire in depth knowledge through further reading and education.

Accounting Basics

General ledger. The company's financial records are maintained in a general ledger, which is a chronological accounting record to keep track of all financial transactions. Transactions are categorized and summarized into general ledger accounts. An account is a unique record for each type of asset, liability, equity, revenue and expense. The number and type of accounts that make up the general ledger is determined by the Chart of Accounts.

The proliferation of financial accounting software is good news for small business owners. In the accounting software, the general ledger works as a central repository for accounting data transferred from all subledgers or modules. The software is usually easy to use, and offers cloud-based options to provide users with easy access from any computer anywhere in the world.

Basic financial statements and reports. The primary purpose of these reports is to give a snapshot of a corporation's financial condition to people outside of the company—investors, bankers, stock analysts and government regulators. In addition, these reports present information in a standard, consistent and familiar format, which make them useful and easy to understand.

For small businesses, accurately tracking financial data is not only critical for running day-to-day operations, but also essential when seeking funding from investors and lenders to grow the business. There are three main financial statements: balance sheet, income statement, and statement of cash flow. Statement of retained earnings is not commonly used but reported.

Balance sheet. The balance sheet reports the amount of a company's assets, liabilities and shareholder's (owner's) equity in a "snapshot" at a given point in time. The report format is structured so that the total of all assets equals the total of all liabilities and equity, which is illustrated in this formula: *Asset = Liabilities + Owner's equity*. This snapshot changes daily as accounts receivable, accounts payables, and inventory are added or reduced. It provides information about the liquidity and capitalization of a business.

- **Assets.** Assets are things the company owns. There are two types of assets: short-term and long-term assets. Short-term assets include cash, short-term investments, accounts receivable, and inventories. Long-term assets include property, factories, vehicles and equipment. Short-term assets are expected to be converted into cash within a year. For long-term assets, the entire purchase costs are not recorded in the year they were purchased, but are rather "spread" over the asset's useful life, which is called "depreciation expense". There are different depreciation methods, and your accountant can help you find the best method for your business.
- **Liabilities.** Like assets, there are both current and long-term liabilities. Accounts payable, notes payable, and accruals are listed as current liabilities because they are expected to be paid within a year. Long-term debt such as bank loans or bonds a company borrows are considered long-term liabilities.
- **Owner's Equity.** Owner's equity refers to the financial stake the owners have in the company. It is represented with the accounting equation: *Equity = Assets − Liabilities.* A business's assets minus the money it owes to others (liabilities) is what is left to the owner(s). This number can be negative if the business owes more than its assets value, which is dangerous if not corrected in a timely manner. For most small businesses, such as proprietor or partnership, owner's equity is shown in the funds invested by the owners as capital contributions, plus retained earnings (i.e., money earned by the business) or subtract losses (i.e., money lost by the business). For corporations that issue stock, the sum of common stock and retained earnings is called "common equity" or "equity," sometimes also called "net worth."

Aileen's Shop for Bookworms Balance Sheet For the Period Ended December 31, 2018		
ASSETS		
Current Assets		
Cash	$5,100	
Debtors	$18,000	
Stock	$3,120	
Total Current Assets		$26,220
Non-current Assets		
Computer	$5,500	
Store Fit Out	$8,100	
Office Equipment	$15,000	
Total Non-current Assets		$28,600
TOTAL ASSETS		$54,820
LIABILITIES AND EQUITY		
Liabilities		
Current Liabilities		
Credit Card	$5,500	
Creditors	$4,120	
Total Current Liabilities		$9,620
Long-term Liabilities		
Total Long-term Liabilities		
Total Liabilities		$9,620
NET ASSETS			$45,200
SHAREHOLDER'S EQUITY		
Owners' Funds		$40,000
Current Year Profit		$5,200
TOTAL SHAREHOLDER'S EQUITY			$45,200

Figure 1. Aileen's Shop for Bookworm Balance Sheet

Income statement. Income statement reports the company's revenues, expenses and profits/losses generated in a given period, typically quarterly or annually. This is usually considered the most important statement as it represents the operational results of the company.

A business can choose to record revenue in two ways—accrual or cash accounting—as its revenue recognition principles. In accrual-based accounting, revenues are recorded when they are earned, not when the company receives the money. In cash accounting, income is reported in the year it is received, and expenses are deducted in the year they are paid. This is based on real-time cash flow. While accrual accounting is more popular as it provides a good overview of a business, retail businesses often use the cash accounting method, which means income and expenses are reported during the reporting period.

Aileen's Shop for Bookworms Profit and Loss Statement For the Period ended December 31, 2018		
Ordinary Income Expense		
Income		
Sales		$52,000
Total Sales		**$52,000**
Cost of Goods Sold		
Opening Stock	$	-
Stock Purchases		$34,320
Less Closing Stock		$3,120
Total Cost of Goods Sold(COGS)		**$31,200**
Gross Profit		**$20,800**
Expenses		
Advertising		$500
Bank Service Charges		$120
Insurance		$500
Payroll		$12,500
Professional Fees (Legal, Accounting)		$700
Utilities & Telephone		$800
Other: Computer Software		$480
Expenses total		**$15,600**
Net Profit before Tax		**$5,200**

Figure 2. Aileen's Shop for Bookworm Profit and Loss Statement

Cash flow statement. Cash flow statement shows the cash inflows and outflows during the reporting period. It is usually broken down into cash flows from three activities: operating, investing and financing. The statements provide a useful comparison to the income statement, especially when the amount of profit or loss reported does not reflect the cash flows experienced by the business. Although many financial numbers can be manipulated, cash flow is a true measure of the health of a business.

There are two closely related terms: cash flow and free cash flow. Cash flow refers to a stream of revenue or expense that changes a cash account over a specified time frame. Free cash flow is cash flow that is available for distribution to investors, which is the basis of a business's value. Free cash flow is the sum of all projects' net cash flow. Net cash flow is discussed later, as it is an important concept when calculating Net Present Value (NPV) when a company makes capital investments.

The importance of cash flow. A company's survival depends on a positive cash flow, and a company's value depends on after-tax cash flows. Small businesses' financial needs are not as complicated as large corporations, but a small business owner needs to pay special attention to cash flow, as it is a true measure of the health of a business.

Aileen's Shop for Bookworms		
Cash Flow Statement		
For the Period Ended December 31, 2018		
Cash flows from operating activities:		
Cash received from customers	$52,000	
Cash paid for expenses	-$15,600	
Cash paid to debtors	-$18,000	
Cash for stock movement	-$34,320	
Cash funded from creditors	$4,120	
Net cash flow from operating activities		-$11,800
Cash flow from investing activities		
Cash paid for property and equipment	-$28,600	
Net cash flow from investing activities		-$28,600
Cash flow from financing activities		
Cash increased in short term debt	$5,500	
Cash increased in long term debt		
Cash proceeds from owners (equity)	$40,000	
Net cash flow from financing activities		**$45,500**
Net Increase in cash		$5,100
Cash balance at the beginning of the year		
Cash balance at the end of the year		$5,100

Figure 3. Aileen's Shop for Bookworm Cash Flow Statement

Key numbers to monitor to run a day-to-day business. Here is an example of the numbers a business owner wants to see every morning to get a pulse on the business: cash in the bank, year-to-date revenues, accounts receivable and accounts payable. Then there are other numbers that are particular to the business owner who sells products: year-to-date purchases, open orders ready to be shipped, backlogged orders, forecasted sales, machine hours that week, billable hours that month, sales leads generated, returns, and customer complaints. Successful companies share their financial position with employees, and many of them design financial reports that are easy to read, and directly linked to the employees' jobs and contributions.

Accounting software. Many small businesses start by using accounting software such as QuickBooks or FreshBooks to set up and manage their books; others hire part-time or full-time accountants. Either way, you are more than likely to use software for the electronic recording, storing, and retrieval of business transactions. Good accounting software allows the users to generate financial statements with a click of a button. The main tasks of using this software include recording all business transactions, organizing expenses, invoicing customers, keeping an up-to-date general ledger, closing the books, and preparing financial statements.

Finance Basics: Making Investment Decisions

As a business owner, you are likely to make major investment decisions. You might want to invest in equipment or plant, acquire another business, or join a franchise. These investments involve large sums of money that affect the company's long-term future. These are perhaps some of the most important and difficult decisions. Thankfully, several analytical tools can measure how that purchase will increase the company's profitability. But before diving into those tools, you need to understand an important basic concept—the time value of money.

Time value of money. The theory behind the time value of money is the idea that a dollar today is worth more than a dollar in the future due to its potential earning capacity. Since money can earn interest, the sooner it is received, the more it is worth. For example, at five percent interest rate, the one dollar coming to you next year is worth 95.2 cents today. So the "present value" for that next-year-dollar is only worth 95.2 cents today, which is the current value of an amount to be paid in the future. The five percent interest rate is also called the discount rate. The discount rate is usually chosen by the analyst who made the evaluation.

Making investment decisions. The essence of investment analysis is this: you discount every future years' cash flows produced by this investment to their present value, add them together, and compare it to your current investment amount. Then you can reach an answer if your investment is going to be worthwhile.

There are different ways to analyze the profitability of an investment; some of the main tools are Return on Investment, Payback Period, Net Present Value, and Internal Rate of Return. All of these can be calculated in a spreadsheet such as Microsoft Excel.

Return on investment (ROI). ROI compares the total cost of an investment with the total amount that it earned during its useful life. For example, if you pay $50,000 upfront cost to invest in a franchise, and the lifetime return is $100,000, the ROI would be 200 percent. The drawback of ROI is it fails to consider the time value of money.

Payback Period. The payback method determines how long it will take for an investment to earn enough cash to "pay back" for the investment, i.e., the initial cash cost. To calculate the payback period, you divide the investment's cost by the amount of cash that the investment is expected to generate on an annual basis. For example, if an investment required $50,000 and it is expected to produce $25,000 of cash flow a year, the payback period would be two years. In this method, cash flows today are evaluated with the same value as cash flows in the future. The major drawback of this method is that it fails to account for the time value of money.

Net Present Value (NPV). In NPV, you calculate the net present value of all future cash outflows (the money you will invest), and cash inflows (the money the investment will produce or cost-savings). Net means you subtract the outflows of cash from the inflows. If NPV is positive, which means more money flows in than flows out, the investment may be worth undertaking. In NPV calculation, future cash flows are considered as discounted cash flows, i.e. NPV considers time value of money. The time of the future cash flows are discounted at an assumed interest rate.

Internal Rate of Return (IRR). IRR is not very commonly used because of its sophistication. It is a discount rate that makes the net present value (NPV) of all cash flows from an investment equal to zero. IRR calculations rely on the same formula as NPV. In general, the higher IRR is, the more desirable the investment is.

This section only gives you a summary and general idea of what to think of when making big investment decisions. When you deal with the future, there is always a risk that your assumptions maybe wrong. As the leader, you must decide how to deal with uncertainties to mitigate and minimize your risks.

Taxes

Every small business faces the tax issue, since you need to meet all the tax responsibilities governed by the Internal Revenue Code, which dictates the specific rules that companies (and individuals) must follow when preparing their tax returns. A business must file federal and state income taxes, and property, sales, and payroll taxes if applicable.

Tax responsibilities and timelines. IRS posts a tax calendar for businesses and those self-employed. The current web address is http://www.tax.gov/calendar, but it may change, so always verify with your accountant. Here is the list of different types of taxes a business is required to file.

1. Annual tax returns. Most annual returns are due April 15. It is the case for sole-proprietor, LLC and partnership companies. A C-corporation must file income tax return Form 1120, which is due the 15th day of the third month following the corporation's fiscal year.
2. Quarterly estimated taxes. The estimated tax payments are due on April 15, June 15, September 15, and January 15 for the prior 3 months. For example, April 15 is the due date for the payment period of January 1 to March 31.

3. Sales taxes are due either monthly or quarterly, depending on the requirement of the state.
4. Employee taxes. When you hire your first employee, you'll need to get a federal employer identification number (EIN) from the IRS if you do not already have one when you started your business. You may also need to get state and local tax numbers. The tax agencies will usually supply you with information about specific payroll tax obligations and the forms you need to use to deposit the taxes and file returns.

Tax deductions. There are also advantages of having your own business in the tax area—deducting business expenses from your top-line revenue to reduce your tax burden. The following business expenses are tax deductible, and it is important that you keep all documents and receipts in case the IRS audits the business. Also remember to check with your accountant as tax laws are updated every year:

1. Employee payroll and most of employee benefits, payment to contractors and freelancers.
2. Business rent or lease payment.
3. Tax such as property tax, state, and local income taxes for business.
4. Interest on business loans.
5. Business losses, which may be carried over to reduce taxable income in future years.
6. Startup expenses—you can choose to deduct up to $5,000 startup costs such as research cost to create your business.
7. Utilities.
8. Advertising, marketing and promotion.
9. Depreciation of property or capital equipment.
10. Software used in business.
11. Service fees such as credit card processing fees.
12. License fees, professional fees, legal and regulatory fees.
13. Employee training and education.

14. Office phone and Internet cost.
15. Insurance premiums for business.
16. All travel expenses, except dining cost is only 50% deductible.
17. Customer entertaining is 50% deductible.
18. Office equipment and furniture.
19. Office supplies.
20. Home office if applicable.
21. Repair and maintenance of your business property and equipment.
22. Vehicle mileage and maintenance used for business.
23. Charitable donations.

Where Do You Find the Money to Start Your Business?

Contrary to popular belief that you need venture capitalists' money to start a business, many successful companies started in the founders' dormitory, basement or garage. They simply start with a bright idea, a passion, and little money invested. When it comes to fund and grow a business, there are numerous funding options. The Entrepreneurship Chapter introduces many reliable ways for both early stage and late stage funding.

On personal debt. Understanding bad debts and their underlying causes is key to financial freedom. Our consumerism society tends to lure you into borrowing to maintain a lifestyle that is too often superficial. Rich Dad Robert Kiyosaki suggests not to carry credit card debt, or any bad personal debt for that matter. Student loans are the most popular form of debt in America, and the topic has appeared in headline news again and again. Carrying student loan delays young people from reaching for their dreams of starting businesses, starting a family or buying homes. Dave Ramsey, author, entrepreneur and financial broadcaster, advises young students to reduce or eliminate student loans through creative ways such as enrolling in local public university, applying various state/federal/college-specific aids and scholarships, and personal funding including savings, working part-time, or simply starting your own business at college.

On Starting your business. It is important to start your own business appropriately. To do so, you will need an accountant, perhaps a lawyer, and a banker if you need to borrow money or plan to borrow money down the road. Although the lawyer and accountant overlap in some areas, an accountant or a CPA could help you to decide the type of business ownership when you first get started, design your accounting system, advise you on how to separate your personal and business expenses, pay taxes correctly, and many other basic accounting functions. In the Entrepreneurship Chapter, I discuss in more details how to get your business started.

References and Suggested Readings

Anthony, R.N., D. F. Hawkins, and K.A. Merchant. *Accounting: Text and Cases.* 13th ed. New York, NY: McGraw-Hill/Irwin, 2011.

Brigham E.F., and M.C. Ehrhardt. *Financial Management. Theory and Practice.* Boston, MA: Cengage Learning, 2014.

Si ciliano, G. *Finance for Nonfinancial Managers.* 2nd ed. Madison, WI: CWL Publishing Enterprises, 2014.

CHAPTER 6

MARKETING: GETTING PEOPLE TO BUY WHAT YOU SELL

> "Marketing is sharing the love you have for your product and service with the people who most want to hear about it, and who most welcome it."
> —Joe Vitale, American author and inspirational speaker

Marketing is the process of turning wants and needs into business decisions and actions. Every successful company must have this main goal: to identify, create, and deliver highly valued products and services to meet customers' wants and needs. Management consultant, educator, and author Peter Drucker says that, "The aim of marketing is to know and understand the customer so well that the product or service fits the customer and sells itself." Successful marketing answers many questions, including who you are trying to reach, how they become aware of what you offer, what story you tell/live/spread, and what makes customers buy. By answering these questions effectively, marketing helps build an emotional connection and trust between the business and its customers.

Small businesses have unique and different marketing challenges than big corporations. Well-known companies usually have recognized brand names that people know and trust. As a result, the marketing strategies that Apple and Nike use do not fit small businesses. During the industrial age, newspapers, magazine ads, and radio and TV commercials were the primary channels a business had to reach customers. Advertising was the privilege of big corporations with huge marketing budgets. However, in the digital age and connected economy powered by the Internet, a small business has access to many new channels to reach potential customers. The digital David can compete effectively with Goliath now. Tools such as email marketing, inbound and content marketing, search engine marketing, and numerous social media channels are just some of the new tools that were not available 20 years ago. These new tools allow people like you and me to reach targeted customers more creatively and cost effectively. It is truly an exciting time to start new businesses.

Broadly speaking, marketing is both the art and science of connecting with customers, building a strong trusted brand, shaping market offerings, delivering value, communicating value, and creating successful long-term growth. This chapter covers basic marketing concepts: marketing plans, market segmentation, market research, competition, pricing, sales and distribution, marketing communications, marketing objective, budget, and measurement.

Marketing Plan

The marketing plan acts as a management tool that can be regularly referred to in order to ensure the business meets its goals, sales targets, and milestones. Good planning requires the business to understand customers and the competition, create values for customers, and outline the ways to reach them. The main component of a typical marketing plan includes the following sections:

- Executive summary: a high-level summary of the plan's content and purpose.
- Description of product or service: What is it? What does it do? How does it fit the customer's needs and wants? What product life cycle stage is it in?
- Value proposition: Why would a customer buy it? What is the value it delivers? What problems does it solve? This requires a two or three sentences of value proposition statement, which is also called an "elevator pitch." It can be as simple as "We help XXX (define your customers) achieve YYY (the value you create for them)."
- Target markets with the support of market research: What markets are currently targeted? What is recommended? Should current target markets be expanded?
- Business environment, industry, and competitive analysis: What are the political, economic, socio-cultural, technological, environmental, and legal (PESTEL) issues in our industry? How is our industry structure functioning under Porter's five forces—competitors, supplier power, customer power, new entrants and substitutes? Who are the major competitors—their pricing, features, benefits, differentiators, and target markets? How do we compare our product/service to major competitors?
- SWOT analysis: Our and each competitor's Strengths, Weaknesses, Opportunities, and Threats.
- Marketing objectives: What are the marketing objectives—building brand awareness, increasing market share, capturing a new target market, increasing revenues and so forth?
- Pricing strategy: What is the best price for our product or service? How does pricing support the marketing objectives?
- Distribution strategy: How do we deliver our product or service—online, retail, distributor, direct sales, or multiple channels?

- Marketing communications: What are the messages and media we use to communicate with our target market? How will our customer become aware of what we have to offer? Which tools will be used to deliver promotional initiatives to each target market?
- Budget and measure: What are the costs for our marketing initiatives and campaigns? How do we allocate the marketing budget to each initiative? How do we measure the return on investment (ROI) of marketing spending?

The following sections outline the steps to generate a successful marketing plan, and each section answers several questions contained in the plan. The steps are also correlated to the famous 4P model in selling physical goods—Product, Place, Price, and Promotions; and the 7P for a service-based business—Price, Promotion, Place, Product, People, Physical evidence, and Process.

Product: Where Do Good Product Ideas Come From?

This section answers the basic questions in the marketing plan: description of product or service and value proposition.

Why do you do what you do? When you develop a new product or service, keep in mind that you are giving energy to it, and it must tie with your passion and intention to serve your customers. It should be about honest work, a personal mission to make something that matters: to solve a problem or add value to someone else's life. In Simon Sinek top-viewed TED talk and his book, *Start with Why, How Great Leaders Inspire Everyone to Take Action*, he explains the "why you do what you do" concept works for both big and small businesses, as well as in nonprofits and in politics. Those leaders who start with why never manipulate, they inspire. And the people who follow them don't do so because they have to—they follow because they want to. The product you offer has to be something in line with your heart's desire, something that will make a difference in the world.

The "Aha Moment." Many entrepreneurs call the moment when they come up with a brilliant idea the "aha moment." Where and how do you find those ideas? You may find them in many places: your expertise area, your inner calling, your passion or hobby, unmet or emerging needs, new ways to solve old problems, and new ways to improve existing products. Products or services come in many sizes and shapes: physical products, properties, software, games, social media apps, books, events, experiences, online courses, life coaching, and consulting, to name just a few.

Starting from a specific niche is one of the most powerful ways to build a successful company. Facebook's Mark Zuckerberg did not start with billions of users; he started by connecting college students with each other. Jeff Bezos started Amazon in his garage when he envisioned the coming Internet revolution. According to Bezos, "The wakeup call [the "aha moment"] was finding this startling statistic that web usage in the spring of 1994 was growing at 2,300 percent a year. You know, things just don't grow that fast. It's highly unusual, and that started me about thinking, 'What kind of business plan might make sense in the context of that growth?'"

Florida teenager Rachel Zeitz transformed her idea and passion into a business. As a lacrosse player, Zeitz didn't like the poor quality and high price of her equipment. So she formed Gladiator Lacrosse at age 13 to make high-quality equipment at affordable prices, turning it into a profitable one million dollar business at age 15. These are just some of the examples of what your "aha moment" might look like. All you need to focus is doing your thing and doing it harder and better than the rest—the recipe for success.

Market research and demand analysis. Market research is an integral part of developing products and services. This requires you to understand what is happening in the industry or segment in which you operate, and how your competitors are making money. Big companies have dedicated teams to perform routine market research. For a small business, the role of market research is to understand why customers will buy your product or service. You can identify customer behavior, including how cultural, social, and personal factors influence that behavior. The typical market research questions focus on who your customers are, what they buy now, why they buy, and what will make them buy from you.

Primary market research refers to the new research carried out by a business itself to answer special questions such as buying motivation. You can conduct a primary market research simply by making phone calls or online surveys with randomly selected members of your target market, or you can study your existing customers, their buying patterns and your sales record.

Secondary market research includes industry reports by government or your trade association or reports published by the research companies in your industry. There are companies selling everything from industry studies to credit reports on individual companies. Online research is also secondary research. For example, if you want to write and market a book, Amazon is a great place for your secondary research; you can find out the top sellers in the categories you are interested in, how the authors market their books, how they design their book covers, and how many books they sell. You can also read customer reviews to give you insights to readers' likes and dislikes.

Value proposition. A value proposition is a statement of how your product or service will benefit your customer. It answers customer questions with clarity and removes their concerns and fears. Customers need to know what they get when they buy your product or service. They ask, "What's in it for me? How much does it cost? Will I save money or time? Will I reduce risk and frustration? Are there potential problems that I need to be aware of? Can you prove it—do you have customer reviews? Why are you better than your competitors?" The human mind is attracted to clarity and transparency. Clarity means to simplify the values you offer so customers can engage; transparency helps build trust so customers can buy. If you confuse, you lose. A simple and effective value proposition example is from WordPress, an online web creation company: "Create your new website for free. WordPress.com is the best place for your personal blog or business site."

Place: Finding Your Core Customers (Target Market)

The better you understand your buyer, the faster your business will gain traction and grow. Who would buy your product or service? Seth Godin says, "If the answer is 'everyone,' start over." You need to clearly define whom you are trying to reach. For example, if you are selling online, you need to find people's online behavior, including which websites or social media sites they like to visit. If you are selling from a retail location, you need to know the demographics of the nearby neighborhood.

Market segmentation and buyer persona. Traditionally, businesses use customer segmentation to narrow down a large target audience to more narrowly defined target groups. The segmentation can be based on demographics, lifestyles, purchasing behaviors, or usage patterns. On the other hand, buyer persona is a semi-fictional character of your ideal customer based on market research and real data about your existing customers. It reveals details of a typical buyer, his or her experiences, goals, preferences, and motivations. For small businesses, segmenting your customers through persona building is a great practice to start with. Once your business reaches a certain scale, you can do more complicated market segmentation through quantitative research on your target audiences.

You can develop a buyer persona by calling and interviewing your existing customers and then construct character profiles regarding the similar behavior, traits, beliefs, attitudes, and values to your product experience. You need to learn what inspires your customers—relationships, healing, travel, culture, movements, winning, competition, knowledge, information, and pain points.

You need to know what they care about, such as being different, doing good works, nurturing or being part of a community. When you interview your best customers, make sure you ask every question related to why they buy your product, how they are using it, what they like and dislike, what other things they might be interested in, their demographic and psychographic status, and their inspirations. These insights will help you and your team to develop messages, stories, and exact words and phrases that resonate with your target buyer.

Great marketers truly understand the psychology of their customers. The biggest benefit of a buyer persona, when done correctly, is to help you identify more accurate, easier and cheaper channels to reach your potential customers.

Here is an example of a buyer persona for a pet care service. The business operates on the first-floor commercial part of a large high-end condominium complex in a big city. The business helps take care of dogs while their owners travel or work. The persona of a typical customer is: Karen, a 33-year-old professional who travels the world for the consulting company she works for. She drives a BMW 3 Series car and loves coffee from the shop next door. She is single and has a cute Shih Tzu. From here on, the marketing channels are identified—a flyer at the coffee bar, an ad on Facebook's pet and animal lovers club, and networking with other single women above 30 who live in the neighborhood.

Build your own tribe and share your movement! In Seth Godin's Book *Tribes: We Need You to Lead Us*, he explains that we all have a basic need to connect with other human beings. The Internet and social networking sites have enabled us to build groups with those who share our passion about something and with those who want to make a difference. See your business as a way to start a movement, build your own tribe, connect with them, and make their lives better.

Competition

Many businesses hate the competition because competitors take away customers who could buy from them. But here is a positive spin: competition is not a bad thing because it validates your product or service. Usually, the more competition, the more opportunity. When you replace scarcity thinking with abundance thinking regarding competition, you open up to new opportunities. You can learn and implement by observing your competition, and you can improve on their weaknesses with even better products or services. There are more than seven billion people on Earth, so anything worth doing has already been done in some way. So don't be afraid of competition. With that said, competition is still tough and poses business challenges. You need to learn how to analyze your industry and competition in order to win in the market place.

The Art of War was written by the famous Chinese military strategist Sun Tzu. Sun Tzu's military theories have been widely adopted by the business world. One the most important principles in *The Art of War* is that in order to win every battle, you need to know both your enemy and yourself extremely well. This is the reason why you need competitive analysis to answer these questions: how is your external business (macro) environment doing? How is the industry business (micro) environment doing? Who are the major competitors in your area? What are their pricing, features, benefits, differentiators, and target markets? How do you compare with your competition in terms of products or services? How do you build a wider economic moat that fends off competition? How do your suppliers, customers, new entrants, and substitutes affect your business? The answers to the above questions are used to identify strengths, opportunities, weaknesses, and threats (SWOT), which will guide your business strategies and decisions.

Several MBA courses (Strategy, Finance, and Marketing) teach analytical tools to study an industry and competition. These tools include PESTEL analysis, Porter's Five Forces, Economic Moat and

SWOT analysis. Established companies have a market intelligence staff to collect and analyze competitive information. Small businesses can also apply these tools in developing marketing strategy.

The PESTEL Analysis. Your business is intricately connected to the outside world, a world that is constantly changing and evolving. A PESTEL analysis is a tool used to analyze and monitor the macro-environmental factors—the external market environment—that have an impact on your business. PESTEL stands for Political, Economic, Socio-cultural, Technological, Environmental and Legal. It helps you identify all those external factors that impact on your business, so you can make informed decisions. Tax policy, employment laws, economic growth, consumer value and preferences, new technology, environmental policies, licensing, and health regulations are some of the important PESETL factors to consider when you start a business.

Within PESTEL, the political, environmental, and legal factors require you to abide by regulations and laws to meet the standards in order to stay in business. The economic factors directly affect your customers' ability and resources to buy your products and services. The socio-cultural factors require you to align with your customers' values, attitudes, and behavior towards your products and services. Technological evolution constantly drives companies to adapt and improve. The company that fails to adapt to change inevitably stumbles.

Porter's Five-Forces. In a competitive market, a business and its rivals compete for business. Porter's five-forces was named after its inventor, Professor Michael Porter. This tool analyzes the five different forces that shape the competition in an industry: (1) rivalry among existing competitors, (2) bargaining power of customers, (3) bargaining power of suppliers, (4) threat of new entrants, and (5) threat of substitutes.

The five-forces provides a deeper dive than PESTEL into industry-specific dynamics. Porter believes the industry structure is what ultimately drives competition and profitability—not whether an industry produces a product or service, is emerging or mature, high-tech or low-tech, regulated or unregulated. According to data from NYU Stern School of Business, each industry has its own established Return on Equity (ROE), which measures profitability by showing how much profit a business generates with the money shareholders have invested. For example, the soft beverages industry's ROE is 28.39 percent, software system and application is 17.08 percent, apparel industry is 7.62 percent, publishing and newspapers industry is -2.51 percent, and total market across all industries is 13.63 percent as of January 2018. This means if you plan to get into the software application business, you might expect an ROE of 17.08 percent.

SWOT analysis. SWOT stands for Strengths, Weaknesses, Opportunities, and Threats. The strengths and weaknesses are internal factors, while opportunities and threats are external factors. A SWOT analysis is usually presented on a one-page document with four quadrants, with a bulleted list in each four areas. SWOT analysis can be done on a business level or product level depending on the strategy it supports. A business can use its strength to take advantage of opportunities and minimize threat, whereas it can take initiatives to improve or eliminate its weaknesses and avoid threats. The business can also select a certain competitor to attack or avoid based on SWOT findings. A good SWOT analysis can lead to actionable strategies. The following table shows a SWOT analysis of an independent neighborhood drugstore.

SWOT Analysis for Chill Pills, a Neighborhood Drugstore

	Helpful	Harmful
Internal	**Strengths** • Well-known high standard customer service for decades • Strong relationship with established customers in the neighborhood • Great location in the high traffic commercial area • Long term rent is reasonable	**Weaknesses** • Space is tight • Inventory cost is high as bank line of credit is low • Inventory software needs upgrade • High health insurance cost for employees
External	**Opportunities** • Launch a frequent buyer program • Good café to make customer stay longer and purchase more • Expand delivery service to more customers farther away • Host health and nutrition education programs to neighbors	**Threats** • Difficult to compete with chain stores with high purchasing power • More confusing direct and indirect remuneration fees • Pharmacy Benefit Managers (PBM) consolidation concerns • Possible increased number of audits and investigations

Figure 4. SWOT Analysis for Chill Pills, a Neighborhood Drugstore

Economic moat. Financial mogul Warren Buffett first coined this idea to refer to a business' ability to maintain competitive advantages over its competitors, and its ability to protect its long-term profits and market share. Morningstar, a leading independent investment research firm, uses five attributes to evaluate the width of the economic moat, also known as competitive advantage. These attributes include Network effect, Intangible assets, Cost advantage, Switching costs, and Efficient scale. For example, Amazon's millions of book buyers gave the company a huge advantage over other eCommerce book retailers and retail bookstores. Its intangible assets include the brand name and consumer trust. Amazon has a cost advantage over others because it can leverage its structural cost advantage and efficiency as it expanded from books to all goods. Although switching cost is low for any retailer, Amazon's first-rate customer service, convenience, and extensive customer review provide consumers peace of mind when purchasing. In

2015, Amazon unveiled a new program geared towards startups called Amazon Launchpad, which helps entrepreneurs "launch, market and distribute their products." Today, many entrepreneurs and authors leverage Amazon's Launchpad as their platform to sell their own brand of products and books. Amazon's operational efficiency, network effect, and laser focus on customer service earn the company a "wide economic moat" status with sustainable competitive advantages.

Your own knowledge on competition. You must have a reason to enter into a specific industry and have some intrinsic knowledge about the industry. Tapping into your own and your network's knowledge will help you understand your competition better.

Final words on competition—making your competitors irrelevant. According to the bestselling book *Blue Ocean Shift* mentioned in Chapter One, "Blue ocean strategists do not take industry conditions as given. Rather, they set out to reshape them in their favor. They do not seek to beat the competition but aim to make the competition irrelevant by capturing new demands." Cirque de Soleil, a Canadian entertainment company is a prime example. It created a new market through reinventing the circus industry. Its profitable customers come from corporate clients and adults who can afford and enjoy live music, and extraordinary theatrical performance of human physical skills.

Pricing Strategy (Price)

The price you set has a subconscious impact on the perceived quality of your product or service and thus its perceived value. People buy based on maximizing the perceived value of what they purchase and act as if the price were equal to quality. Pricing strategy is always tricky, as much an art as it is a science. Many entrepreneurs either overestimate their ability or feel less valuable than the price the customers are willing to pay. One entrepreneur who teaches people how to operate online stores recounted his story. In the beginning, he charged a low price for his course and his students got poor results. He decided to triple the price, and the results of his new students were spectacular. Why? By charging a higher price, he got more serious students who were committed and worked harder, which is the recipe for success. Stephen Kenn sells specialty furniture and leather goods. Kenn developed amazing film-quality videos to strike an emotional cord with customers. His $1,000 leather bag sold out fast because the bag was transcended to something beyond a mere product and became a symbol of a boy's memory of his lost father as a war hero.

Pricing methods. There are many ways to set pricing. Here is a quick list to refer to:

1. Perceived-value pricing. This strategy uses marketing to enhance the perceived quality and desirability of the product. Some educational insiders revealed that many private universities set high tuition fees to demonstrate their prestigious status.
2. Value pricing. Value pricing combines higher quality and lower price to maximize perceived value. Southwest Airlines and Ikea are good examples.
3. Target-return pricing. This is the simplest one, building a profit margin into the price.
4. Going-rate pricing. This strategy targets the competitors' pricing in order to meet or beat their prices.
5. Discounts and allowances. The business gives price reductions for paying early, paying in cash, buying in quantity, trading in old products when buying a new one, and a variety of discounts and allowances.
6. Special financing, payment terms, and warranties. These terms are often designed to facilitate purchases, such as one full payment at a lower price or several separate payment options at a slightly higher price.

7. Customer-segment pricing. Different prices are offered to different groups of customers.
8. Channel pricing. The same product is offered at different prices at different locations.
9. Barrier pricing. This is to set the price so low that it will discourage new entrants, but it could also ruin the business. It is not suggested for a small business.
10. Loss-leader pricing. Use low prices to attract buyers or drive traffic to a store or online purchase.
11. Optional-feature pricing. This refers to additional prices for "extras." Today many airlines charge an extra price for seats in the front of the airplane or seats with extra legroom.
12. Two-part pricing. A fixed fee is charged to participate, augmented by additional charges based on usage.
13. Product-bundling pricing. This amounts to offering a discount when a collection of products is purchased together.
14. Popular pricing. Starting with discount deadline and raise prices gradually.

Small businesses usually do not have economic scale to achieve low unit cost, so competing on low price is not a recommended option. Many successful entrepreneurs suggest using perceived-value pricing by setting a higher price. When you start a business out of love and passion, you want to create an image of quality, so you are better off pricing your product at least in the middle or upper-middle of the accepted price range in your product category. Then, give buyers something additional—over-deliver on your promise, extra products, extra service, convenience, or a money-back guarantee to increase the perceived value of the deal.

Sales: Delivering Value to Customers

One of the oldest sayings in business is "Nothing happens until somebody sells something." Manufacturers can't manufacture, accountants can't count, and finance can't process paychecks unless there is money in the account. Every employee in your company needs to understand the point of view of those in sales. Additionally, as an entrepreneur, it is extremely important to learn the art of selling. You need to develop your skills in selling in the areas of negotiation, cold calling, pitching ideas, reaching decision makers, and closing a sale. Even working in a traditional job requires interview skills, which is a process of selling your own expertise and value, the ability to get a job to begin with.

Sales and marketing. Established companies have carefully crafted distinctive sales and marketing roles. Typical sales roles, especially in selling high-price items, involve in-person meeting, demonstration, negotiation, and closing. Of course, networking, making phone calls, and building relationships with prospective customers are also important parts of the job. Traditional marketing roles involve market research, product design input, pricing, and reaching and communicating with potential customers through advertising, public relations, online, and social channels.

The massive buying shift. As entrepreneur Marcus Sheridan wrote in his book *They Ask, You Answer*, both consumer and business customers' buying patterns have gone through a monumental shift over the past decade, and the line between sales and marketing has been completely blurred, if not totally erased. Prospects are making as much as 70 percent of the buying decision before ever reaching out to a company.

Today's many successful small businesses are uniting sales and marketing. Ian Altman, an experienced sales strategists and keynote speaker, pointed out that in the old days, companies saw marketing and sales as two distinct roles. The Marketing Team was there to create interest and awareness. The Sales Team was to build customer confidence and urgency. "As more of the buying process continues to shift to online, we have a huge opportunity to build customer trust and uncover urgency through content [marketing]. Smart companies use online content as an integral part of the sales process. The content serves as examples to help your clients better understand how you address common challenges they might be facing." The sub-title of *They Ask, You Answer* promises "a revolutionary approach to inbound sales, content marketing, and today's digital consumer." The book shows how much impact honest and transparent content can have on today's buyers and ultimately alter the sales process, and how sales and marketing can work collaboratively to create incredible results.

Marketing Communications and Branding

Marketing communications refer to how your business attempts to inform, persuade and remind customers about your products or services. A marketing communication tool can be anything that promotes and spreads the word: advertising, personal selling, direct marketing, word-of-mouth, sponsorship, events and experiences, promotions, and public relations. The best communication is based on your understanding of your customer's pain points, aspirations, beliefs, fears, internal and external needs, and psychological needs. Good marketing communication helps build trust, connections, authority, empathy, clarity and simplicity.

Branding. A brand is the set of expectations, memories, stories, and relationships that, taken together, account for a consumer's decision to choose one product or service over another. Customers usually associate a brand with a story. Seth Godin, entrepreneur and author of many marketing best-selling books says, "The marketer's job, then, is to tell a true story, one that resonates, one that matters to people, and to repeat it often enough that it creates value." Successful brands such as Apple, Nike, and Tesla connect with their customers emotionally; they stand for authenticity, uniqueness, talent, high achievement, and helpfulness. They mean something to their customers, and they would be missed if gone.

Communications channels. Before the 1990s, marketing, especially consumer marketing, was synonymous to advertising, and thus ad and promotion campaigns were synonymous with marketing communications. However, the Internet has changed the promotional landscape. The once-powerful TV, radio, newspaper, and magazine advertising spending are diminishing, perhaps only relevant to some businesses. Today, Internet and digital marketing provide a more level playing field for small business to compete with the big brands. However, with this change comes information overload, and buyers are increasingly difficult to reach. Marketers are using a variety of digital marketing platforms such as inbound marketing, content marketing, search engine marketing, and social media marketing. Seth Godin commented:

> The Internet is the first medium invented in 100 years that wasn't invented to make advertisers happy. The connection between running ads and making money is broken, probably forever. As soon as you take that out of the equation, everything we understand about marketing, manufacturing, distribution—it all goes away. The new era of modern marketing is about the connection economy, it's about trust, it's about awareness, it's about the fact that attention is worth way more than it used to be. Attention doesn't come in nice little bundles anymore.

"They ask, you answer" business philosophy. As previously discussed, modern entrepreneurs like Marcus Sheridan have pioneered a different marketing and communications strategy to attract customers and build trust. Marcus is a partner of River Pools and Spas, a swimming pool company in Virginia serving customers in the states of Maryland and Virginia. While facing imminent bankruptcy as the aftermath of the 2008 recession,

Marcus started online content marketing by using the "They Ask You Answer" principle. He offered candid and transparent answers to every customer question he had encountered in his sales career. Each customer question was turned into an educational blog or a video posted on his company's website. His website was the first to give comprehensive and trustworthy answers in cost/pricing, problems, competitive comparison, and customer reviews. His company literally became the "Wikipedia of pools," with hundreds of educational blogs, videos and eBooks. In six months, his company prospered while competitors were closing shops. Before recession, his swimming pool company spent about $250,000 in advertising to achieve gross sales of about $4,000,000 (six percent). In 2011, it only spent $18,000 in marketing and reached gross sales of roughly $5,000,000 (less than one percent) in the middle of the great recession. Marcus's new way of marketing not only saved his company but also established him as a renowned consultant, speaker, and author. The story is captured by his eBook *Inbound and Content Marketing Made Easy,* and his print book *They Ask You Answer.* His honest and transparent way of marketing impacted buyers and changed the sales process for good.

Why does They Ask You Answer work? The content River Pools and Spa created not only attracts strangers who search on the Internet, but also facilitates the whole customer buying decision process. While giving prospective customers full education, the content helps remove and disarm objections, concerns, and fears of making wrong choices. Every industry needs such a company. The questions that your customers ask can be the guiding post of your content creation.

Entrepreneurs now creatively use many other forms of communications. Every couple of years, new tools become popular: online blog and email marketing in the early 2000, podcast and social media surge around 2005, inbound/content marketing around 2012, and Facebook ads, YouTube channels, and video blogs in recent years. Many new entrepreneurs built their success by focusing on quality content on selected channels to reach their target customers, building trust and connections.

Build your own media list. Email marketing is said to be one of the most effective marketing methods, providing a ROI of 39, which means you put $1 in email marketing, you are likely to earn $39 in return. Some say an email address is worth $1 per month, which means if you have 10,000 email addresses who opted to receive your message willingly, you could have an income of $10,000 a month, a $120,000 annual income. Email marketing works like advertising. While advertising uses TV, radios and magazine's media lists, you build your own media list through email—your own followers.

Today's digital marketing and web analytics are getting closer than ever to a science. Split testing (also referred to as A/B testing or multivariate testing) applies statistics in email marketing and website performance. It is a method of conducting controlled, randomized experiments with two variants, A and B. The goal is to improve a website performance metric, such as clicks, form completions, opt-in, and eventual purchases.

Marketing Budget and Measurement

An important part of the marketing function is to set clear marketing goals. Marketing budgets and measurements can then be aligned with those goals. If you have several goals, it is helpful to put them in order of priority. Today's digital technology has made marketing measurement easy. For example, many marketing software programs can track each marketing initiative's performance in real time with accurate data about generating awareness, attracting, engaging, nurturing, conversion and revenue. Marketing is now converging art and science.

Marketing budget. A common question new business owners ponder is, "how much do I spend on marketing?" According to the Gartner CMO (Chief Marketing Officer) Spend Survey in

2017-2018, marketing counted for about 12 percent of company revenue in 2016, and about 11 percent in 2017. Some marketing agencies use this marketing math: for established companies that have been in business more than five years, the typical marketing spending is 5 to 12 percent of gross revenue. For new companies, the spending is 12 to 20 percent of gross revenue. While the percentage seems high, new companies need to develop market awareness and build brand trust and recognition with a new audience. Of course, these are general rules that have to be adjusted for different businesses.

Measurement tools. Once you've outlined your strategies and identified your tactics, you must create your measurement protocol. Without measurement, you will not know how your marketing performed and how you can improve. Each business situation is different, so the focus and measure can be different. Some of marketing key performance indicators (KPI) for most businesses include the following:

1. Revenue. If you have multiple sales channels, revenue should be measured across each channel. If you have multiple distribution channels including web, events, and dedicated sales, the measure of the revenue from each channel versus the cost should be an indicator of each channel's efficiency.
2. Cost of customer acquisition (CCA) and customer's lifetime value (CLV or CLTV). CCA refers to the cost to find, convince, and onboard a new customer. CLV predicts the total net profit a company makes from any given customer. CLV must be above CCA to provide a profit.
3. Sales leads generated from sources including content marketing, word-of-mouth referrals, online referrals, social media, email marketing, paid search (Google pay-per-click), organic search, and direct website traffic.
4. Conversion rates and web analytics. These numbers are important digital marketing metrics that give insights into

your website's visits, page performance, social media metrics, blog hits, video hits, as well as about who is visiting and why and what the visitor has viewed or read. Many marketing automation software programs can track and measure these performance indicators. Google offers free Webmaster tools to track many of these metrics.

5. ROMI. Return on marketing investment (ROMI) is the profit contributed by marketing minus marketing spending, divided by the marketing spending. According to the generally accepted accounting principle, marketing is not considered an investment because it is expensed in the current period—this is in comparison with capital expenses such as plants and inventories, which are depreciated over a period of time. ROMI can also be measured by different marketing tactics. For example, Facebook offers a tool called Insights to track ROI and social impact.

6. Net Promoter Score (NPS). Companies such as Disney and my alma mater Jack Welch Management Institute adopted NPS to measure performance. NPS claims to be correlated with revenue growth. One of the key questions to calculate NPS is "how likely is it that you would recommend [this brand] to a friend or colleague?" While any score above 0 is good, anything above 50 is "Excellent" and above 70 is "world class."

Once the marketing goals and KPIs are defined, you need to gather this performance information on a weekly, biweekly or monthly basis. You can compare the results with goals and history data for easy decision-making.

In summary, most MBA programs focus on the basic, generic approach to marketing: appealing to wide demographics using the four P's—product, price, place, and promotion. Designed for the industrial age, the mantra for business was "we made this, how do we get people's attention?" As a result, many average products were sold through good advertising. Today, when customers are equipped with more information, marketers really need more advanced skills, such as developing product ideas that fulfill unmet needs in the marketplace; honing in on a target audience through both traditional and digital marketing; and constantly analyzing, measuring, testing, and improving marketing capabilities.

References and Suggested Readings

"The Best Ways to Do Market Research for Your Business Plan." https://www.entrepreneur.com/article/241080.

Godin, S. *Purple Cow: Transform Your Business by Being Remarkable.* New York, NY: Portfolio, 2007

Kim, W. C. and R. Mauborgne. *Blue Ocean Shift: Beyond Competing. Proven Steps to Inspire Confidence and Seize new Growth.* New York, NY: Hachette Books, 2017.

Kotler, P. and K. L. Keller. *A Framework For Marketing Management.* 5th ed. Upper Saddle River, NJ: Prentice Hall, 2012.

Patel, N. "What Marketing Channel Should You Start with First If You're a Brand New Business?" *Neilpatel.com.* http://neilpatel.com/blog/what-marketing-channel-should-you-start-with-first-if-youre-a-brand-new-business/

"Return on Equity by Sector (US)." http://pages.stern.nyu.edu/~adamodar/New_Home_Page/datafile/roe.html.

Saltzman, J. "Why Competition Is Good." *Entrepreneur.com.* https://www.entrepreneur.com/article/239043

Sheridan, M. *They Ask You Answer: A Revolutionary Approach to Inbound Sales, Content Marketing, and Today's Digital Consumer.* Hoboken, NJ: John Wiley & Sons, Inc., 2017.

CHAPTER 7

OPERATIONS MANAGEMENT: GETTING THINGS DONE MOST EFFICIENTLY

"Operations management is the fundamental gut of how a company operates. It's the ability to deliver products, the ability to source products, the ability to design services, it's everything that gets from your suppliers to you to the customer. It's every element of it, and it's what you do every day."
—Jack Welch, the former chairman and CEO of GE (1981–2001), author and founder of Jack Welch Management Institute

Operations management (OM) refers to the processes and procedures that a business uses to convert materials and labor into products or services. It is how a company gets from an idea of a product or service to its ability to source, design, and deliver them to customers.

OM is what a business does every day. Whether you're running a law firm, a hospital, a manufacturing business, or an online store, business comes down to the efficient delivery of high-quality goods and services to the customer. The essence of good operations management is to create the highest possible level of efficiency, improve quality and service, and reduce cost.

For most businesses, a large percentage of revenue is spent in the OM functions. Good operations have a profound effect on profitability and productivity. For a business to be successful, operations must have well integrated links with all the other functional areas: strategic planning, marketing, sales, accounting, and finance. There must be formal integration even if all of these functions fall under one or just a few people.

There are significant differences in operations between a mature, established organization and a startup company. Large companies can afford detailed analysis and lengthy planning, while entrepreneurs speed up decisions through experience, gut feelings, and quick calculations. However, the basic components of OM are similar:

- Align operations with business mission and strategy
- New product or service development
- Inventory management
- Supply chain management
- Logistics
- Purchasing
- Manufacturing
- Distribution
- Quality system and continuous improvement

Although OM sounds complicated, there's a silver lining—entrepreneurs and small start-ups can design and implement new and innovative operations processes without historical burdens and outdated ways of doing things. Older, larger businesses are always looking for ways to cut costs and improve operations. Small firms are fast and flexible and can quickly gain the upper hand over the competition if they can deliver more efficiently.

That's one of the reasons why Amazon, only started recently, has outperformed big retailers' efforts in online business and continued to excel in operations.

Mission and Strategy – Guiding Post of Operations

Mission, vision, and strategy have appeared in multiple places throughout this book. They are like the North Star of a business, guiding and seeping into all areas of business.

Mission. A mission helps you know where your business is going. A mission is your organization's purpose—why you exist and what you contribute to society. Smart leaders use mission statements so everyone in the company is clear on the direction of the company. For example, Facebook's mission is to give people the power to build community and bring the world closer together. This mission statement appeals to customers, stockholders, and employees.

Strategy. A strategy is an organization's action plan to achieve the mission. A business can choose to achieve its mission in several conceptual ways: differentiation, cost leadership, response, and niche-focused. Therefore, operations need to deliver products or services that are better or different, cheaper, faster, or more narrowly focused than the competition.

Competing on differentiation. To differentiate a business is to be unique. Uniqueness can be physical characteristics or experiential services. Differentiation can be achieved by innovative design, service quality, and distinctive experience. For example, a Louise Viton bag charges 100 times or more than a no-name bag. Disney offers more magical experiences than a local county fair.

Niche-focused. Focus on niche is an effective differentiation strategy for small businesses. Niche means that a business selects a narrow segment of the market to sell to. This requires intense understanding of both the marketplace and customers. For example, Lefty's is a store that focuses on the ten percent of the population that is left-handed. It offers left-handed school supplies, kitchen goods, gardening tools, and custom gift sets both online and through its retail store at San Francisco's Pier 39.

Competing on cost. Walmart is a great example of a company competing on low cost by offering no-frills practicality. Its slogans from the beginning have been "Always Low Prices" and "Save Money, Live Better." Walmart achieved its low cost by deploying a sophisticated OM system. Cost leadership was achieved by low overhead, effective capacity use, and efficient inventory management.

Competing on response. Response refers to flexible response, quickness, or reliability of scheduling. FedEx is a company that promises "When it absolutely, positively has to get there overnight" and "The World on Time." Amazon Prime Now offers everyday household items and essentials with a free two-hour delivery.

With the guidance of mission and strategy, an operations plan has to cut through the clutter and simply state how the organization will satisfy its customers and drive profitability. The plan needs to answer tactical questions such as: How do we design our new products and services? How will we source our suppliers? How will we manage our inventory to get to our customers? How will we control purchasing? Does the same department or person control distribution? Which shipping company do we use?

New Products and Services Design

Innovative new products are the fuel of business growth. All products go through a life cycle of introduction, growth, maturity, and decline. Throughout the life cycle, a new product generates negative cash flow in the introduction phase due to research and development costs and marketing expenses. The product contributes the most profit during the growth and maturity phases, when customers accept the product and sales continue to grow. Eventually a product dies and newer products replace it. The Walkman personal

CD player is a great example of a product that has gone completely through its life cycle.

New products development requires cash, an understanding of the customer and the marketplace, and necessary human talent. The process starts with strategy, idea generation, feasibility study (idea screening), concept development and testing, product and marketing plan creation and evaluation, and introduction to the market. It is important that operations must be integrated into the early stage of product development. A typical product development includes the following stages:

1. Concepts: generate ideas from many sources.
2. Feasibility: screen the ideas, verify if customers will understand or need the product or service, and check if the company has the ability to carry out the idea.
3. Requirement: define customer requirement so the customer will buy the new product.
4. Functional specifications: define how the product will work.
5. Product specification: specify how the product will be made.
6. Design review: confirm if the product specifications are the best to meet customer requirements.
7. Test market: verify if the product meets customer expectations and if customers are willing to "vote with their wallets."
8. Launch: introduce new product through education, promotion, and channel decisions.
9. Evaluation: measure if the product or service is a success; reflect on what you have learned.

DMADV. Some big corporations follow Six Sigma's DMADV, a methodology to develop new products with built-in quality systems. Six Sigma is a careful, analytical thought process of solving problems using data. This is the system that drives defects down to less than 3.4 per million opportunities. DMADV stands for Define, Measure,

Analyze, Design, and Verify and is based on data, early identification of success, and thorough analysis.

A small business can learn the essence of such a system, which is to minimize the occurrence of flaws in products and services. However, the DMADV methods are only useful when they are based on a long and stable operating history, which startup companies do not have. For entrepreneurs, the lean startup method helps reduce failure rate and move with speed.

Lean Startup. The lean startup is a concept first coined by entrepreneur and author Eric Ries. The key concept is to get customer feedback quickly and often and to eliminate uncertainty in the product development process. In his book *The Lean Startup, How Today's Entrepreneurs Use Continuous Innovation to Create Radically Successful Businesses*, Ries advocates rapid scientific experimentation and "validated learning" to study what customers really want, to continuously test business visions, shorten product development cycles, adapt and adjust quickly, and prevent failure.

Inventory management

Inventory is cash sitting in products, but it serves an important purpose—to have products available for customers to purchase. For many companies that sell physical goods, inventory is one of the most expensive assets, representing as much as 50 percent of total invested capital. While you can reduce costs by reducing inventory, customers can become dissatisfied when the item they want to buy is out of stock. Imagine you walk into an Apple store and fancy the latest iPhone; you would certainly be disappointed if the product were out of stock. Inventory management strikes a balance between investment and customer service, so the business knows how much to order and when to order.

A typical manufacturing company's inventory has four types: raw material inventory, work-in-progress inventory, maintenance/

repair/operating supply inventory, and finished good inventory. A service company can be quite different from this model; some examples of inventory include hospitals having patients waiting for service at the ER, seats on the airplane, hotels rooms, staff, food, and beverages.

Inventory serves several functions in a successful business:

1. Meet customer demand: maintaining finish goods inventory allows the company to immediately fulfill customer's purchases, even during fluctuations of demand.
2. Decouple various parts of the production process. When a company's supplies fluctuate, extra inventory might be necessary to decouple the production process from suppliers.
3. Take advantage of quantity discounts: purchasing either raw material or finished products in large quantities may reduce the cost of goods and their delivery.
4. Hedge against inflation, supply shortage, and upward price changes.

Inventory management. Inventory management is the practice of overseeing and controlling the ordering, storage, and use of components that a company uses in producing the products it sells. It is also the practice of overseeing and controlling of quantities of finished products for sale.

ABC analysis. Pareto principle (named after Vilfredo Pareto, a 19th-century Italian economist) is also known as the 80/20 rule. It states that roughly 80 percent of the effects come from 20 percent of the causes. ABC analysis is the application of Pareto principle in product sales. A is the most valuable items, while C is the least valuable ones. Class A refers to the top 10-20 percent of the products that generates 70-80 percent of revenue; class B are those 30 percent of products that generate 15-25 percent of revenue; and class C, which might only represent five percent of revenue, could take up to 30-55 percent of inventory volume. Applying ABC analysis can help the business achieve a healthy inventory level, drive down working capital, and better design cycle counting and reorder frequency.

Inventory management software. If your business is in the retail or online retail space, you most likely need inventory management software to organize your product and vendor information, create and submit accurate purchase orders, improve speed and accuracy, record sales, facilitate physical inventory count, and reconcile differences. Software can automate the bulk of the inventory management. If inventory is an important part of your business, educate yourself on this topic. Amazon is perhaps one of the best companies in the world in inventory management. Learning from best practices is a great way to increase your leadership and management capability; inventory management is no exception.

Supply chain management

Supply chain management refers to the coordination of all supply chain activities starting from the raw material and ending with a happy customer. Thus, supply chain includes suppliers, manufacturers, warehouses, service providers, distributors, wholesalers, and customer-facing retailers or facilities. For instance, a restaurant's supply chain must be fast and good, otherwise the customer won't be fed on time, or worse, gets food poisoning.

Define a sourcing strategy. When you sell products, you need to decide whether to make the product or outsource the product. For example, if you plan to sell yoga mats with your own brand name, you can choose to open a factory and make the mat yourself or buy it from an established manufacturer and just add your logo. The latter is obviously a better choice for entrepreneurs with limited capital. Since your supplier is an integral part of your business, it is important that you manage the relationship, product quality, and delivery with clearly defined standards.

One of the prime examples of outsourcing manufacturing

is Nike, a company that markets athletic footwear and apparel. Nike owns no factories; instead, its manufacturing is outsourced to third parties due to the cost advantages. Most raw materials in Nike's supply chain are sourced to the manufacturing network of hundreds of factories in tens of countries. As a result, supply chain management and delivery precision in a company like Nike is critical to ensure the customer receives the right product on time.

Now back to the yoga mat. Ryan Daniel Moran started selling yoga mats made by Chinese manufacturers he found on Alibaba.com. Moran designed his own extra thick, extra-long and environmental friendly yoga mat, added his own logo and packaging, did the drop shipping to Amazon, and let Amazon handle the rest. He built a multi-million-dollar lifestyle business with his first two yoga products.

Building the suppliers base. Suppliers (aka vendors) must be selected and actively managed. Some of the factors when choosing a supplier include strategic fit, supplier competency, delivery, and quality. At the end of the day, your business success is about providing high quality products or services and making sure that your customers are happy. Supplier selection is usually a four-step process:

1. Supplier certification. International quality certifications such as ISO 9000 and ISO 14000 are indicators of a company that follows sound quality and environmental management standards. Some large companies even create their own supplier certification program.
2. Supplier development. The supplier must have an appreciation of quality requirements, product specifications, schedule, delivery, and procurement policies.
3. Negotiations. Most business-to-business transactions are negotiated not only on the price itself but also on credit and delivery terms, quality standards, and other factors.

4. Contracting. The goal of contracting is collaboration. Some common features of contracts include quantity discounts (the bigger the order, the lower the price), buybacks (especially in books and the magazine business), and revenue sharing (sharing risks of uncertainty by sharing revenue).

Logistics and delivery. Logistics and delivery determine the efficiency of operations through integrating all material acquisition, shipping, and storage activities. The main questions are: Will warehousing and delivery services be performed in-house or outsourced? What are the delivery channels? What is the most important in terms of time, cost and reliability when choosing a shipping system—trucking, railroads, airfreight, water, or multiple forms?

Some business owners build their business by using Amazon's advanced logistics and delivery system. The Fulfillment by Amazon program manages the logistics such as unpacking, warehousing and shipping for third party sellers—people like you and me selling products through Amazon. All the business owner needs to do is to prepare the products and ship them to Amazon's warehouses.

Actively manage the supplier and distribution network. In today's interconnected business, competition is no longer between companies but between supply chains. The key to supply chain success is to collaborate with members on both supplier and distribution channels so the whole supply chain is benefited. Conscientious business owners follow principles, standards, and ethics such as positive supplier and customer relationships; sustainability and social responsibility; protection of confidential and proprietary information; and conforming to applicable laws, regulations, and trade agreements. When a business outsources its manufacturing to third world countries, there is a potential to offload pollution to suppliers or choose suppliers that hire child labor. A business must rigorously analyze its supply chain to uncover its risks and weaknesses and prepare an overall risk management and resilience plan.

Quality (and Continuous Improvements) as a Competitive Advantage

Product quality is essential for a company's success in the marketplace. Quality improvement can help a business increase in sales and reduce costs, and both can increase profitability. Increase in sales often occurs when the business improves its reputation for quality products or services. High product quality also allows the business costs to drop due to increased productivity and lower rework, scrap, and warranty costs. One study found companies with the highest quality were five times more productive than companies with the lowest quality.

The media frequently reports on product recalls issued by companies in car manufacturing, consumer electronics, food, and medicine. While a large car manufacturer can afford billions of dollars of loss in recalls, a product recall can severely impact small businesses financially. The key to improve quality is to build a culture of quality and integrate it into everything from inventory to employees.

Quality system. A quality system allows a business to satisfy its customers and obtain a competitive advantage. A good quality strategy begins with an organizational culture that fosters quality, followed by an understanding of the principles of quality, and ultimately engages employees in the necessary activities to implement quality. Startups and new businesses have a certain advantage because they can learn best practices from direct competition or other great companies in various industries.

Your basic quality plan should answer these questions: What are the organizational goals? How will processes be monitored and controlled? Who will be assigned with the authority and responsibility for quality throughout the organization? How do we build a quality-oriented company culture? What results are expected?

Total quality management (TQM). TQM is a management approach that emphasizes quality to achieve long-term success and customer satisfaction. It involves the entire company from supplier to customer. In a TQM effort, all members of an organization participate in improving processes, products, services, and the culture to ensure their organization is operating in the most efficient way possible. Here are some of the high-level TQM concepts:

1. Continuous improvement. Large industrial companies such as Toyota reaped big profits and high product quality by initiating projects such as Lean, Rapid events, Kanban, Six Sigma, and other process improvement tools, including PDCA (plan-do-check-act), workout, DMAIC, and Optimize.
2. Six Sigma. Six Sigma was championed as a set of management techniques to improve business processes by greatly reducing the probability of an error or defect. It is designed to lower costs, save time, and improve customer satisfaction. An analogy to Six Sigma would be if one million passengers pass through an airport with checked-in baggage each month, a Six Sigma program for baggage handling would result in only 3.4 passengers experiencing misplaced luggage. According to Bureau of Transportation Statistics, the 2015 number was 3.24 per *thousand* passengers, which is almost 1,000 times more error in comparison to the Six Sigma standard.
3. Employee empowerment. This is the ongoing process of providing the tools, training, resources, encouragement, and motivation your employees need to perform at the optimal level. It means involving employees in every step of the process. Employees who work in the process on a daily basis understand the weaknesses of the system or process. The freedom, flexibility, and power to make decisions and solve problems leave an employee feeling energized, capable, and determined to make the organization successful.

4. Benchmarking. Benchmarking is a practice to establish baselines and define best practices inside or outside of your industry. The goal is to identify improvement opportunities, create a learning environment, and improve and grow the business. For example, Zappos' celebrated customer service can be the benchmark of call centers. Zappos depends on its outstanding customer service to encourage its customers to trust, engage, and stay loyal to its brand—a smart marketing move.
5. Just-in-time (JIT). JIT is designed to produce and deliver goods just as they are needed. It cuts inventory cost, improves quality, and offers better inventory control. The result is the efficient use of working capital and enhanced cash flow. Toyota and McDonald are great examples using JIT service.
6. The Toyota production systems (TPS). The TPS obviously was credited to Toyota Motors. The system has three components: continuous improvement, respect for people, and standard work practice. It allowed Toyota to keep low inventory levels, allow employees to work intelligently, and eliminate waste.
7. Lean operations. Lean operations means identifying customer value by analyzing all the activities required to produce the products and then optimizing the entire process from the customer's perspective. Lean drives out all waste that adds no value to the customer. For example, defects, overproduction, waiting, transportation, excess inventory, motion waste, and excess processing are all considered waste as they do not add value from the view point of the customers.
8. Lean Six Sigma. This combines Lean and Six Sigma concepts. It is a collaborative team effort to improve performance by systematically removing both waste and variation.

Operational excellence. Operational excellence provides

many opportunities for a business to improve profitability, quality, service, productivity, efficiency, and innovation. A great business is also a learning organization that continuously finds better ways to do things in every aspect and every corner. The employees are empowered to ask, "How can I do better than what I am doing now?" "How many sales calls did I made a day?" "How efficient were my sales calls?" "How long does it take to close the books in finance?" "How can I get better analysis on sales, marketing, and manufacturing so that we can do better?"

In summary, operations management is a vital component of every organization. The role and responsibilities may vary depending on the type of business, the industry, and the life stage of the organization, but its importance does not. Every organization, product manufacturer or service provider, for-profit or non-profit, government or private, all have the need to effectively produce and deliver their products or services to satisfy the customers and investors. Every business plan needs to include a detailed and well-developed operations plan, and every business owner should have an understanding of the role of operations for long-term and scalable growth.

References and Suggested Readings

Garner, S. "What Is Operation management?" *Canadianentrepreneurtraining.com.* http://canadianentrepreneurtraining.com/what-is-operations-management/

Heizer, J. and B. Render. *Operations Management. Sustainability and Supply Chain Management.* Peason. Upper Saddle River, NJ, 2014.

Master, N. "Amazon's Inventory Management Secrets." *Regen.com.* http://www.rfgen.com/blog/bid/246924/amazon-s-inventory-management-secrets.

Novak, S. "Operations Management and the Startup Company." *Innovationforgrowth.co.uk*. http://www.innovationforgrowth.co.uk/Blog/operations-management-and-the-startup-company/

Ries, E. *The Lean Startup*: *How Today's Entrepreneurs Use Continuous Innovation to Create Radically Successful Businesses*. Crown Business. New York: NY, 2011.

The American Society for Quality. *http://www.asq.org*.

American National Standards Institute. *http://www.ansi.org*.

CHAPTER 8

MANAGERIAL ECONOMICS: MAKING DECISIONS IN THE FACE OF CONSTRAINTS

> Economics is everywhere and understanding economics can help you make better decisions and lead a happier life.
>
> —Tyler Cowen, an American economist and professor

Each of us has limited resources, since we do not have the time or the money to do everything we might want to do. So we must make a decision—out of all the possible options, how do we choose to spend our time and money? Tony Robbins famously said, "Where focus goes, energy flows." Economics is the study of how people make their decisions and choose that focus. Economics also studies how our motivation to acquire more resources affects the decisions we make.

At its simplest, managerial economics is about making decisions at the individual, family, business, government, and market levels in the face of such constraints as scarce resources, pricing pressures, or global competition. A business always operates in the macro and micro economic environment at the same time. Macroeconomics studies the decisions made by countries and governments and current trends in economic sectors such as manufacturing and housing. It also explores powerful concepts like government output, money, expectations, supply and demand, market structures, the government's role in markets, and forms of competition.

Microeconomics studies the economics at an individual and a business level, a small subset of macroeconomics. Understanding both macroeconomics and microeconomics is important for a business to achieve success. This knowledge of its economic environment can help a business analyze and master competitive forces at both a quantitative and practical level.

Macroeconomics

Major macroeconomics principles govern the world economy. Macroeconomics examines the larger scale economies on a global or national level and reports on issues such as economic growth, monetary and fiscal policy, inflation, interest rate, and unemployment.

Macroeconomic forces affect all of us in our daily lives. For example, inflation influences the rise in prices we pay for goods and services, and, in turn, the value of our income and savings. Interest rates determine the cost of borrowing, such as the rate of bank loans for our business or the mortgage rate when we buy a house. Exchange rates affect the price we pay for imported products in stores.

Macroeconomics forecasts commonly reported in the media include predictions on consumer spending, business investment, home building, exports, imports, gross domestic product (GDP), unemployment rates, and interest rates. These indicators are used to predict the health of the current economy and the future of the economy. Although economic forecasting is troubled with uncertainty even by the most experienced economists, we still need this knowledge to help make important decisions such as new product introductions, product pricing, or hiring.

Ray Dalio, an investor and founder of one of the world's largest hedge funds, made a popular 30-minute animated YouTube video on Economics 101: *How the Economic Machine Works*. The video has been viewed by millions of people. It answers the question "How does the economy really work?" The video breaks down economic concepts like credit, deficits, and interest rates, allowing viewers to learn the basic driving forces behind the economy, how economic policies work and why economic cycles occur.

David Moss, a Harvard Business School professor, wrote the book *A Concise Guide to Macro Economics* for business people and students to understand important macro concepts. He explains that macroeconomics rests on three basic pillars: output, money, and expectations.

Output. The most widely accepted measure of national output is gross domestic product (GDP). GDP is the heart of macroeconomics. It is the market value of all the final goods and services produced within a country's borders over a given time period. Simply put, a whole country's economic output is summarized as GDP. Governments typically divide expenditure on final goods and services into five categories: consumption by household (C), investment in productive assets (I), government spending on goods and services (G), exports (EX), and imports (IM). The formula is:

$$\text{National Output (GDP)} = C+I+G+EX-IM$$

The amount of output a country produces (or its amount of output per capita) determines its level of prosperity. Per capita GDP takes GDP and divides it by the number of people in the country. The per capita GDP is especially useful when comparing one country to another, because it shows the relative performance of the countries.

Although a country may temporarily consume more than it

produces, it can do so only by importing more goods and services than it exports and by borrowing from foreigners to finance the difference. All the cross-border transactions are accounted for in a country's balance of payments.

Money. Money is used to pay for goods and services and to pay people for their work. The most vital role money serves is as a medium of exchange. Money also serves to store value and serves as a unit of account in which books are kept and prices quoted. Money affects variables such as interest rates, exchange rates, and the aggregate price level (inflation). In general, when money supply increases, it drives down interest rates, increases inflation, and depreciates exchange rate. But macroeconomics is not an exact science, so general rules can be violated during a financial crisis and certain events.

Expectations. According to Professor David Moss, expectations about the future play a pivotal role in an economy, as they can drive an entire economy in a positive or negative direction and can even become self-fulfilling. For example, if businesses in general become pessimistic about future demand by canceling investment projects and laying off workers, they can cause a reduction in aggregate demand. As consumers cut back on spending because of layoffs or expectations of job uncertainty, the businesses would cut down investment further, thus creating a self-fulfilling downward spiral. When this occurs, GDP falls, unemployment rises, and prices tend to decline. The exact opposite can happen: when businesses are optimistic about the future, they can drive demand beyond the true productive capacity of the economy or even overheat the economy. One of the main jobs for macroeconomic policy makers such as a central bank is to manage expectations.

To appreciate macroeconomics, you can access many sources of economic forecast information from the following:

1. The National Bureau of Economics Research, Inc. (NBER), a non-profit organization publishing research from leading scholars in the field.
2. Federal Reserve Economic Data (FRED). FRED is a government source.
3. Manufacturing Industry Productivity Database, patent data, imports and exports, and IRS information. These are all industry data.
4. Resources for Economists (RFE) on the Internet. RFE offers a broad array of business and economic forecasting resources.
5. Leading business publications such as *The Wall Street Journal, Business Week, Forbes*, and *Fortune*.

In summary, the world is always changing, always going through ups and downs. Understanding macroeconomics theory provides us with a framework to understand economic events and the shape of the business environment that we are in. In turn, the knowledge affects the risks and rewards of business and personal investment decisions we make every day.

The recent recession, triggered by the financial crisis in late 2007, resulted in many corporate bankruptcy filings and closures. Numerous sources of investment and financing dried up. However, the rapid increase of layoffs, the availability of newly unemployed workers and a shortage of employment choices created a large increase in entrepreneurship. In Robert Fairlie's research published in *Strategy + Business, How the Great Recession Spurred Entrepreneurship*, the author showed that higher local unemployment rates were tied to higher rates of entrepreneurship. The unemployed started more businesses than those who held a job. Despite decreased GDP, shortage of money supply, and gloomy expectation held by many, plentiful small businesses started by prosperity-conscious entrepreneurs flourished.

The advice here is that if you have unique ideas, passion,

perseverance, hard work, and high self-expectations, you can create your own economy, where money will be available to you, and business will prosper. This will be another whole new topic we can explore in future books.

Microeconomics

Microeconomics focuses on the decisions made by individuals and businesses regarding the allocation of resources. It looks at how a specific company could maximize its production and capacity, so it could lower prices and better compete in its industry. It studies supply and demand and other forces that determine price levels in the economy. For example, if you were a manufacturer of tennis clothes and accessories, you would want to know how many pieces of a given attire will consumers purchase? At what price? What are the other factors affecting quantities and prices? How sensitive are consumers to changes in price? When the economy takes a nosedive, how will consumers respond? Do they buy more because they have more time to play? Do they cut back because they have less income? Or do they just wear cheaper clothes to play?

Government policies can alter the inputs and incentives for an individual's economic decisions. These policies include tax policy, fiscal policy, regulations, tariffs, subsidies, legal tender laws, licensing, and public-private partnerships. They manipulate the costs and benefits that individuals face in nearly every facet of modern life. Sometimes the impacts of government policy are intentional. For example, the U.S. government provides multi-billion dollar subsidies each year to farmers who grow corn. As a result, the corn production is very high—although the policy is controversial; why not subsidize non-GMO and organic vegetables? On the other hand, the government can put a tax on cigarettes and alcohol to discourage behavior that it doesn't approve of. Other impacts are unintentional. When the government propped up minimum wages, for example, it unintentionally raises the menu price in restaurants and grocery stores and made some businesses less willing to hire extra employees. On the other hand, raising the minimum wage boosts broad-based aggregate economic demand and reduces the poverty rate.

Basic Microeconomics Concepts

Here we examine some of the key concepts in microeconomics: utility, supply, demand, market equilibrium, and government interventions.

Utility. In economics, utility refers to a person's overall happiness and satisfaction. Economics assume that we all allocate our resources and make decisions to maximize our utility, i.e., to achieve maximum happiness. The law of diminishing marginal utility means that the first unit usually has a higher utility than every other unit that follows. For example, eating the first ice cream cone makes you happy, while each additional one has lower utility. You might even reach negative utility, perhaps a stomachache or a sugar high after a third or fourth cone.

Opportunity cost. Opportunity cost is the cost we pay when we give up something to get something else. An idea begun by John Stuart Mill, opportunity cost refers to the benefit, profit, or value of something that must be given up to acquire or achieve something else. For example, if you decide to stop working and go back to the university for an MBA degree, your opportunity cost is losing your job and a paycheck. Even though that decision has a big opportunity cost, you believe an MBA degree will give you more job opportunities and higher salary after graduation.

Demand. Demand refers to how much a product or service is desired by buyers. Holding all other factors constant, an increase in the price of a good or service will decrease demand, and vice versa. Several factors can cause a shift in demand: changes in consumer preference, changes in income levels, changes in the price of other goods, changes in consumer expectations, and changes in the number of consumers in the market.

Supply. Supply represents how much the market can offer. The supply for a good is how much of that good producers would produce at various prices. Holding all other factors constant, an increase in the supply of a good or service will decrease its price and vice versa. Several factors can cause a shift in supply: changes in cost of production, changes in opportunity costs, changes in supplier expectations, and changes in the number of suppliers.

Supply and demand are related. Higher prices tend to reduce demand while encouraging supply, and lower prices increase demand while discouraging supply. Let's look at banana supply and demand as an example. In one year, the weather is perfect for bananas. The growers have a great harvest. This increases the supply of bananas. In order to sell the perishable crop, the growers reduce the price because there are so many more bananas on the market. In the next year, there is a terrible pandemic in the plantations, and the amount of bananas produced is reduced dramatically. The growers raise the price—assuming the demand stays the same—but there are now much fewer bananas available to sell.

A small startup business and its consumers are too small to influence the supply and demand of a market. The key question is—will there be enough demand for what the new business intends to supply? That's a critical question and, if the answer is negative, the business cannot be successful.

Market equilibrium. Market equilibrium is a market state where the supply in the market is equal to the demand in the market. The equilibrium price is the price when the supply equals the demand in the market.

Government interventions. Although government interventions distort the market, they are sometimes justified and supported by society. Price floors and ceilings and tax and subsidies are two examples of government intervention.

Price floor and price ceiling. In some cases, the government imposes a minimum price on a good, a "price floor." For example, the U.S. Department of Agriculture (USDA) administers the price floor for milk, setting it at $0.10 per pound. In other cases, the government imposes a maximum price on a good, a "price ceiling." For example, some local government use "rent control," a form of price ceiling, to limit the amount a property owner can charge for renting out a home or an apartment.

Taxes and subsidies. Many goods are taxed or subsidized by the government. The tax increases the price paid by consumers, reduces the revenue received by suppliers, and reduces the quantity transacted. For example, in 2018, President Donald Trump introduced billions of dollars in new tariffs on Chinese imported goods. China retaliated by announcing tariffs on U.S. imports. Tariff is a tax, so the government will see increased revenue from imports. Local industries also benefit from a reduction of competition, since import prices are artificially inflated. But tariffs could also potentially hamper the economy and bring pain to consumers as they pay for higher prices on everyday products.

A subsidy reduces the price paid by consumers, increases the revenue received by suppliers, and increases the quantity transacted. A subsidy is a benefit given by the government to groups or individuals, usually in the form of a cash payment or a tax reduction. The subsidy is typically given to remove some type of burden, and it is often considered to be in the overall interest of the public. For example, the U.S. government gives cash subsidies to farmers so that they can sell at a low market price but still achieve financial gain in a highly competitive international industry. As of 2018, the Australian government provides $10,000 wage subsidies to companies that hire employees who are 15-25 years old, over 50 years old, or indigenous Australians.

Cost of production. Business owners need to understand a company's costs, such as marginal cost, fixed cost, and variable cost.

Marginal cost refers to the cost added by producing one additional unit of a product or service. For example, one car plant makes 300,000 cars per year. If producing an additional 10,000 cars requires building a new factory, the marginal cost of the extra cars includes the cost of the whole new plant.

Fixed cost refers to business costs that are constant regardless of the quantity of goods or services produced. Fixed costs usually include rent, insurance, and licenses.

Variable cost refers to the cost that varies with the level of output. For example, buying tires, battery, and other necessary components are variable costs for car manufacturers.

Market structures. Capitalism is an economic system where private individuals and businesses own the means of producing and distributing goods, lands, technologies, utilities, and services. Capitalism needs a free market economy, and competition is the regulatory mechanism of a free market. Different forms of market structures such as perfect competition, monopolies, oligopolies and monopolistic competition are some of the features of capitalism.

Perfect competition. *Investopedia* defines perfect competition as a market structure in which these five criteria are all met:

1. All firms sell an identical product;
2. All firms are price takers—they cannot control the market price of their product;
3. All firms have a relatively small market share;
4. Buyers have complete information about the product being sold and the prices charged by each firm;
5. The industry is characterized by freedom of entry and exit.

No market is perfectly competitive, but some are closer to the ideal than others. For example, agricultural commodities, such as oranges, are the classic example of perfect competitive market. Stock markets and debt markets are also perfect competition.

Monopoly. When there is only one supplier in a market, that supplier has what is known as a "monopoly." The most common monopoly markets operate with exclusive license, anti-competitive subsidization and/or tariff protection. For example, public utilities such as water, natural gas, electricity, and telecommunications are monopolistic markets.

Unlike companies in a perfectly competitive market, a monopoly can raise the price of the good it sells without immediately losing all of its sales. In the U.S., the government gives pharmaceutical companies patent monopolies on drugs and allows them to charge any price during the 20 years of patent time. Although the government chooses to do this as a way to spur innovation, when the protected drugs charge hundreds of times of the free market price, a problem exists.

Oligopoly. An "oligopoly" is an industry dominated by a few companies, with barriers to entry that make it difficult for new companies to enter the industry. For example, phone service companies in the U.S. are dominated by AT&T, Verizon, Sprint, and T-Mobile. An oligopoly is similar to a monopoly, except that rather than one firm, two or more firms dominate the market. There is no precise upper limit to the number of firms in an oligopoly, but the number must be low enough that the actions of one firm significantly impact and influence the others.

An oligopoly in which participants openly engage in price fixing is a cartel. The Organization of Petroleum Exporting Countries (OPEC), a group consisting of 12 of the world's major oil-exporting nations, is one typical example. Cartels often fail due to the incentive that each party wants to cheat. Most jurisdictions have laws against price fixing and collusion. In many countries, antitrust laws prohibit cartel behavior.

Monopolistic competition. The monopolistic competition defines a common market structure in which firms have many competitors, but each one sells a slightly different product, not a perfect substitute.

Many small businesses and restaurants operate in the monopolistic competition structure. In the case of restaurants, each one offers something different or something unique, but all are essentially competing for the same customers. Barriers to entry and exit in this type of industry are low, and the decisions of any one business do not directly affect the others. Monopolistically competitive businesses are assumed to be profit maximizers because they tend to be small, with entrepreneurs and owners actively involved in managing the business.

Global Economic Trends and Challenges

The world's economies are becoming increasingly interconnected. Take the example of the 2007-2009 recession, one of the worst recessions in 80 years. Recession is defined as a downturn in economic activity, characterized by at least two consecutive quarters of decline in a country's GDP. The blame was pinned on the U.S. housing bubble, and the inadequate government oversight of U.S. financial institutions, which lured people to buy homes they could not afford. These financial institutions created many risky and complex instruments called mortgage-backed securities, collateralized debt obligations, and credit default swaps. These assets were bought by many investors across the financial system and investors worldwide. As a result, the U.S. housing collapse quickly spread overseas, and problems were transmitted to European countries and beyond.

While the speculative and risky behaviors of homebuyers, property investors, and financial institutions are to blame, some scholars raised the global issue. Kellogg's *Insight* journal published an article based on the research of India professors Ravi Jagannathan, Mudit Kapoor, and Ernst Schaumburg. The professors argued that the housing bubble was partially fueled by globalization, and the U.S. dollar was as much to blame as banks. They pointed out the economic growth in the developing world, technological advances, and globalization in the labor supply of workers from these countries generated a large amount of new wealth. Without domestic financial markets capable of absorbing the wealth, the money flowed into the U.S. real estate, which, in turn, partially fueled the U.S. housing bubble.

Global economy and labor supply. The information age is affecting all business areas—supply chain, information and communication technologies, global market access, and changes in organizational structure. There is also a massive shift in the labor supply to the developing countries. Today a small business owner can hire an experienced programmer in India to build a website or a mobile app for as low as a couple of hundred dollars, a small fraction of what they would pay for a local marketing agency. NASA was able to design a robotic arm component for $50 through Freelancer.com. An experienced architect in Italy designed a three-story house in the U.S. for $150. The Internet has unleashed the power of the global workforce.

The world population trend. University of Toronto academic David Foot, the best-selling author of *Boom, Bust and Echo: How to Profit from the Coming Demography*, famously said "demography explains two thirds of everything." The global population trends are clear: in developed countries, people live longer, family size shrinks, and fertility rates decline, resulting in an older population. For example, the economy of Japan is the third largest in the world by nominal GDP and the fourth largest by purchasing power parity. The World Health Organization (WHO) predicted that by 2025, 30 percent of Japan's population will be aged 60 years or older, while the overall population is falling due to low fertility rate. According to the Tokyo Times, the adult diapers market is expected to surpass the baby diapers market by 2020. As a result, the country's economy is shrinking and unable to depend on an expanding labor force to drive growth. So are the trends for most western European countries. The United Nations report warned Japan first and the world second that the working-age population ratios are declining steadily. This trend has put enormous burden on public healthcare, social welfare, and economic prosperity. On the other hand, a German study by IIASA researcher Elke Loichinger found that an aging population offers many benefits, including increased education levels, less consumption of energy resources, sharing wealth, better health, and quality of life.

The trend is different in the developing countries where the fertility rates remain high, which adds to new pressures on immigration, urbanization, climate change, public health, and security. Other challenges include unemployment, environmental degradation, food and water shortages, failing states, and inevitable disasters.

Sharing economy. Embodied by Uber and Airbnb, the sharing economy is rapidly producing platforms that permit consumers to gain temporary access to various assets. People are sharing rides, apartments, workspace, boats, equipment, and even fashion. According to a BCG survey, the top three benefits consumers enjoy are: variety, access to better products and services, and the ability to have a unique experience.

Employee-free society and many new forms of entrepreneurship. The author, speaker, and entrepreneur James Altucher raised this idea. He pointed out that more than 200 years ago the concept of an employee did not exist. The rise of corporatism created employees. The baby boomer generation was perhaps the last generation to hold one job for decades in factory systems and company towns. The once stable corporate life has turned to disorder, especially after the dot-com bubble in 1995-2001 and the recession in 2007-2009. On September 20, 2015, *Fortune* listed the largest layoffs by U.S. corporations from 1993-2015. The average downsizing was 30,000 to 60,000 employees. These companies are all huge corporations like IBM, Citi, Sears, GM, AT&T, Ford, Kmart, Circuit City, Boeing, and the Bank of America.

On the other hand, entrepreneurship is playing a vital role in the growth of the U.S. economy. In fact, it is entrepreneurship and innovation that really fuel economic growth. In the U.S., entrepreneurship has always been part of American identity and self-image. Ed Sappin wrote in the *Entrepreneur* magazine, "Entrepreneurs create businesses, businesses create jobs, and people with jobs make good customers. New and growing businesses represent the principal sources of job creation and innovative activity in an economy, two factors that generally result in the rising standards of living for all."

Not only are traditional entrepreneurs enabled by the digital economy but also are solo entrepreneurs, lifestyle entrepreneurs and freelancers, all part of a new worldwide social trend. It is never been easier to start a business than today. According to the *Entrepreneur* magazine, "solo-preneurs" are a powerful and growing force in today's career landscape. A solo-preneur is "a business owner who works and runs his or her business alone." Lifestyle entrepreneurs are those who create a business with the purpose of altering their personal lifestyle and not for the sole purpose of making profits. A lifestyle entrepreneur focuses more on the life rewards, and have a passion for what they are doing. Both types of entrepreneurs are what Altucher calls "choosing yourself"— living outside the comfort zone and always focusing on the future, personal freedom, and the power of now.

The Fast Company reported the freelancer economy has been on the rise. Talent-matching platforms and co-working spaces are two of the leading trends behind a freelancer economy that is growing increasingly more robust. An Intuit study estimated that by 2020, more than 40% of the American workforce, or 60 million people, will be independent workers—freelancers, contractors, and temporary employees.

Consumer trends. *Euromonitor International,* a market research firm for global consumer trends, pointed out that today's consumers are savvy, hyper-informed, and highly skeptical. They have the opportunity to compare prices at their disposal, and they are less bothered about labels and recognized brands. Consumers are shopping on value and novelty, flitting between shops and products.

> Consumers are now more demanding of products, services and brands than ever before and are using digital tools to articulate and fulfill their needs…. They want safety in a perceived volatile

world, particularly for their nearest and dearest, and look to tech tools as aids in this quest. They want to shop faster and secure the swiftest convenience.... Consumer requirements even extend to the post-purchase experience; to their relationship with brands once the transaction has happened.

Younger "consumers in training" have a voice that goes beyond "pester power" (the ability of children to pressure their parents into buying them things). This gives them a more active role in what is purchased, often turning them into in-house shopping consultants. Consumers aged over 50, the most vocal and youngest of whom are part of a generation known for their outspoken views— the baby boomers—are themselves living a changed ageing narrative with articulate "ambassadors" and organizational advocates with greater faith in their abilities and purpose.

In summary, the world, especially the business world, is complex and difficult to predict. All economic predictions and models have limitations. Managerial economics seeks to explain why and how an individual or an organization should direct scarce resources and manage cost effectively. However, successful entrepreneurs own their future, create their own economy, and thrive in an unpredictable world. You can be one too.

References and Suggested Readings

Dalio, R. "Economics 101: How The Economic Machine Works" https://www.youtube.com/watch?v=PHe0bXAIuk0
Fairlie R.W. "How the Great Recession Spurred Entrepreneurship."

Strategy + Business. https://www.strategy-business.com/article/re00240?gko=d3750

Frakt, A and M. Piper. *Microeconomics Made Simple.* Simple Subjects, Colorado, 2014.

"The Intuit 2020 Report. Twenty Trends That Will Shape The Next Decade." http://http-download.intuit.com/http.intuit/CMO/intuit/futureofsmallbusiness/intuit_2020_report.pdf

Jagannathan, R., M. Kapoor, and E. Schaumburg. "What Really Spurred the Great Recession?" *Kellogg Insight.* https://insight.kellogg.northwestern.edu/article/what_really_spurred_the_great_recession

Kasriel-Alexander, D. "Top 10 Global Consumer Trends for 2017." *Euromonitor.com.* http://go.euromonitor.com/rs/805-KOK-719/images/wpTop10GCT2017EN.pdf

Moss, David. *A Concise Guide to Macroeconomics.* 2nd ed. Cambridge, MA: HBR Press, 2014.

Sappin, E. "7 Ways Entrepreneurs Drive Economic Development." *Entrepeneur.com* https://www.entrepreneur.com/article/283616

Schrader, B. "Here's Why The Freelancer Economy Is On The Rise." *Fast Company.* https://www.fastcompany.com/3049532/heres-why-the-freelancer-economy-is-on-the-rise

Wallensteain, J. and U. Shelat. "Hopping Aboard the Sharing Economy." *Boston Consulting Group.* https://www.bcg.com/publications/2017/strategy-accelerating-growth-consumer-products-hopping-aboard-sharing-economy.aspx

CHAPTER 9

STRATEGY: A CUSTOMIZED PLAYBOOK TO WIN

> "Process improvement programs are like teaching people how to fish. Strategy maps and scorecards teach people where to fish."
> —Robert S. Kaplan, an Emeritus Professor of Leadership Development at the Harvard Business School

Business strategy can be viewed as a customized playbook to help the business win in the marketplace. Strategy offers a holistic view of the business, a big picture by looking at a business's internal capabilities, customers, competitors and the external environment. Good strategies lead to business growth, sustained competitive edge, and strong financial performance.

Leaders need the skills to understand and develop strategies. Many published strategy books are highly academic and difficult to understand. Jack Welch outlined the most simple yet effective three-step process to do strategy in his book *Winning*. The steps are: (1) come up with the "big aha" for your business—a smart, realistic fast way to gain sustainable competitive advantage; (2) put the right people in the right jobs to drive your big idea forward; and (3) relentlessly seek out the best practices to achieve your big idea, and then find ways to continually improve those practices. According to Welch, "In real life, strategy is you pick a direction and implement like hell."

Step One: The "Big Aha" and How to Win

Many entrepreneurs credit their beginnings to that "aha" moment, the moment that sparked a sudden insight or discovery of an unmet need or a process innovation. These entrepreneurs find brilliant ideas when their minds are quiet and relaxed; and some even schedule time to practice silence and solitude through meditation, hiking in nature, and other forms of relaxation. Everyone, including you, comes with a precious gift, and has something to offer to the world. As Laura Sandefer says beautifully in her book *Courage to Grow*, we can all begin the hero's journey to answer the call to adventure in this life.

Jay Papasan, the bestselling author who wrote the forward to Pat Flynn's book *Will It Fly, How to Test Your Next Business Idea so You Don't Waste Your Time and Money*, identified a common myth of starting a business. Instead of the commonly accepted equation: IDEA + EXECUTION = SUCCESS, he suggests YOU + IDEA + EXECUTION = SUCCESS.

Papasan and Flynn want you to do a gut check—why do you do what you do? Does it fulfill you? Does it align with your passion, an inner calling to build something or serve someone? These questions are vitally important before you start your first business. That's why "YOU" comes before "IDEA."

Fuzzy Yellow Balls is a company founded by Will Hamilton and Adam Sieminski to create the ultimate destination for recreational tennis players who seek the highest quality instruction from the biggest names in the game. Its website and YouTube videos offer numerous free tennis lessons to millions of visitors, and the company's income comes from paid membership by loyal customers. This is yet another great example of two people starting with a passion and, through consistent work, launching an online business that results in getting paid well by doing something they love.

Vision and mission. After your great business idea is sparked from the "aha" moment, you need to develop a strong vision and mission to guide the business. As discussed in the Operations Management chapter, vision and mission state the fundamental purpose of the company, values, and view of the future.

A vision is a simple statement of where a business is going and what its leaders want it to be in the future. A mission defines the company's business, its objectives, and its approach to reach those objectives. Simply put, it explains the company's reason for existence. For example, Amazon's mission is "to be earth's most customer-centric company, where customers can find and discover anything they might want to buy online, and endeavors to offer its customers the lowest possible prices."

Understanding the external business environment. The external environment includes the forces outside the business that are beyond a company's control. Tax policy, employment laws, competition, licensing and regulations, industry structure, and profit are some of the important factors to consider when you start or operate a business. These factors impact each business and industry differently, and you need to learn how they apply to yours.

Several MBA courses such as Marketing and Finance teach you how to analyze the external environment. In the Marketing Chapter, I have explained PESTEL, Porter's five forces, economic moat, and SWOT analysis. These useful analytical tools can be applied to a big corporation, an individual product line, or a small business. Of course, the angles are different in each situation. They help you gain a clear picture of how to balance the opportunities and risks associated with dynamic and uncertain changes in the business environment.

Understanding the internal business environment. The

internal environment refers to the company's internal factors that impact its operations and success. Strategic leadership, resources and capabilities, and strengths and weaknesses relative to competitors are the three internal factors that result in good or bad performance.

Strategic leadership. Leaders and managers play critical roles in managing the business, making choices and decisions, and deploying resources and capabilities. The importance of strategic leadership is further discussed in step two of this chapter—the right people to implement strategy. The following illustration shows the stewardship of strategic leadership in a business:

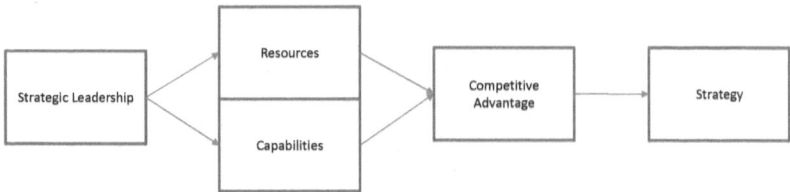

Figure 5. Strategic Management Concepts

Resources, capabilities, and the VRINE model. Resources and capabilities are the fundamental building blocks of an organization's strategy.

Resources refer to the inputs that a business uses to create goods and services. Tangible resources are physical. They are land, employees, money, and inventory. Intangible resources are non-physical. They are leadership quality, innovation, culture, patents, trade secrets, service, and brand reputation. These intangible resources play critical roles in the customers' buying decisions, as buyers are subconsciously affected by intangible benefits they perceive in their minds.

Capabilities, also known as competencies, refer to an organization's skills to use resources to create goods and services. Core competencies are the capabilities and skills that distinguish a business from its competitors. They are the foundations upon which businesses grow, innovate, and deliver value to customers.

The VRINE Model. VRINE stands for Value, Rarity, Inimitability, Non-substitutability and Exploitability. The model is illustrated in the book *Strategic Management* by Professor Mason Carpenter and Professor Wm. Gerard Sanders to evaluate resources and capabilities. Here are the evaluation criteria:

- Value: a resource must add value to meet demand in the market or protect the company from uncertainties.
- Rare: scarce resources not widely possessed by competitors can add competitive advantage.
- Inimitability and non-substitutability: these are resources that are difficult for competitors to imitate, substitute, or reproduce. Until other competitors can normalize the advantages, the company can achieve above normal profits for an extended period of time.
- Exploitable: companies can actually exploit the above four features to achieve competitive advantage and improve profitability.

Resources and capabilities that meet the VRINE criteria help companies gain significant competitive advantages and achieve superior performance. In the real business world, a company needs to modify, upgrade, reconfigure, acquire, or divest its resources and capabilities constantly. The abilities to adapt to change and proactively initiate change are critical to long-term business success.

Jack's famous five slides for strategy. Jack Welch developed a straightforward approach to define and implement an organization's strategy in order to sustain a competitive advantage. The following five slides come from Jack and Suzy Welch's book *Winning*. The steps they outlined paint a clear and comprehensive picture of how a business competes in the market place. It worked wonders in a vast company like GE but can be adapted to small businesses too.

Slide #1: What the playing field looks like now?

- Who are the competitors—large and small, new and old?
- Who has what share, globally and in each market? Where do you fit in?
- Is your business commodity or high value or somewhere in between? Is it long cycle or short? Where is it on the growth curve? What are the drivers of profitability?
- What are the strengths and weaknesses of each competitor? How good are their products? How much does each one spend on R&D? How big is each sales force? How performance-driven is each culture?
- Who are this business's main customers, and how do they buy?

Slide #2: What the competition has been up to?

- What has each competitor done in the past year to change the playing field?
- Has anyone introduced game-changing new products, new technologies, or a new distribution channel?
- Are there any new entrants, and what have they been up to in the past year?

Slide #3: What you've been up to?

- What have you done in the past year to change the competitive playing field?
- Have you bought a company, introduced a new product, hired a competitor's key salesperson, or licensed a new technology from a start-up?
- Have you lost any competitive advantage that you once had—a great salesperson, a special product, a proprietary technology?

Slide #4: What's around the corner?

- What scares you most in the year ahead—what one or two things could a competitor [or a new player] do to nail you?
- What new products or technologies could your competitors launch that might change the game?
- What merge and acquisition (M&A) deals would knock you off your feet?

Slide #5: What's your winning move?

- What can you do to change the playing field—is it acquisition, a new product (to gap what's missing), globalization?
- What can you do to make customers stick to you more than ever before and more than to anyone else?

These five slides are action-oriented, and provide a comprehensive view of the business strategy for the leader. Slide 1 presents an accurate snapshot of today's players in the industry. Slide 2 helps to understand the competition and their strategies. Slide 3 looks at your own business strategies and implementation. Slide 4 lets the strategic leader predict potential threat and disruptive forces. Slide 5 makes you think of your own winning moves.

Creating strategy—which generic strategy to choose? The purpose of business strategy is to generate superior value for customers. As I have covered in the Operations Management chapter, there are two main generic strategies that can be implemented in any industry and in companies of any size: *low cost* or *differentiation*, while *response* and *focus* are two subsets of the differentiation strategy.

1. **Low-cost leadership.** Low-cost leadership means a business uses low cost as a competitive advantage. Cost leadership is achieved by delivering an acceptable product that satisfies basic needs at the lowest possible cost. IKEA is a prime

example of this strategy. The company offers stylish furniture at the lowest price to attract customers. Thrift is in its company culture. IKEA works hard to cut costs in every function from design, manufacturing, transportation, to marketing. IKEA requires the customers to pick up flat-packed modular furniture to assemble at home. Customers are happy to get the furniture right away, while saving the cost of delivery.

2. **Differentiation.** Differentiation means a business offers products or services that are valued and perceived by its customers as unique and better than the competition—to the point that customers will pay premium prices. A business usually chooses to add costs in order to add more value, and charge sufficiently higher prices to offset the additional cost. To implement this strategy, a business tends to invest heavily in research and development, build a strong brand, and use effective marketing and sales strategies.

The famous entrepreneur, marketer, and best-selling author Seth Godin uses the "purple cow" analogy for differentiation: "A Purple Cow is a product that is so different from the others around it that it stands out, like a purple cow in a field of brown ones." To differentiate a business is to be unique like a purple cow. The uniqueness can be physical features or experiential service. Whole Foods Market is a top-tier national chain that offers local and organic wholesome food. Zappos delivers "wow" through service by becoming a customer-obsessed company. Differentiation can be achieved by innovative design, service quality, experience, focus and speed.

Focus on niche **as a differentiation strategy.** Focus means a business selects a narrow segment of the market—a niche in which to sell its products and services. Successful implementation requires intense understanding of the marketplace, the customers, and competitors. Seth Godin recommends that the marketing strategy for a niche-focused business should be telling a true story, one that resonates, one that matters to people, and one that is repeated often enough that it creates remarkable value. Adopting *focus* as a differentiation strategy is an effective way for a small business to compete with big companies. Here are two examples. Warby Parker was founded by four students whose aim was to offer designer eyewear online at a revolutionary low price, while leading a way as a socially conscious business. For every pair of glasses the company sells, a pair is distributed to someone in need. A food photographer Dana created Minimalist Baker, a site that shares plant-based recipes requiring 10 ingredients or less, one bowl, and 30 minutes or less to prepare.

Response **as a differentiation strategy.** Response refers to flexibility, quickness or reliability of scheduling. FedEx and Amazon Prime Now covered in the Operations Management chapter are two perfect examples of fast response strategy.

Strategy diamond. This is a tool developed by strategy researchers Don Hambrick and Jim Fredrickson. It shows the five key parts of a strategy: arenas, vehicles, differentiators, staging and pacing, and economic logic. By answering the questions in each of these areas listed in the graphic below, you can paint a clear big picture of your business in the market place.

Figure 6. Strategy Diamond

Step Two: The Right People to Implement Strategy

Jack Welch says, "Any strategy is dead on arrival unless a company brings it to life with people—the right people." At the end of the day, it is the people—the leaders, managers and employees who execute the strategies and deploy resources and capabilities. The importance of people has been discussed in detail in the People Management chapter. Again, let us remember Jim Collins's timeless quote: "First get the right people on the bus and the wrong people off the bus, and then figure out where to drive it. 'First who then what' you can more easily adapt to a changing world."

Strategic leadership. Strategic leadership is a key internal business factor. A strategic leader such as a CEO or a business owner spends time not only in strategy and implementation but also plays many other roles: interpersonal role as the leader, figurehead, and liaison; informational role as the monitor, information disseminator, and spokesperson; and decision role as entrepreneur, disturbance handler, resource allocator, and negotiator.

Jim Collins discussed the level 5 leadership concept in his book *Good to Great: Why Some Companies Make the Leap and Others Don't*. He concluded that the great companies (11 out of the 1,435 publicly traded companies his team studied) had Level 5 leadership in key positions, including the CEO, at the pivotal time of transition. Collins defines level 5 leaders as those who display a powerful mixture of personal humility, and indomitable will on top of all the other effective and basic leadership qualities. These leaders are incredibly ambitious, but their ambition is first and foremost for the cause, for the organization and its purpose, not for themselves. While Level 5 leaders can come in many personality packages, they are often self-effacing, quiet, reserved, and even shy. Every good-to-great transition in Collins's 11 winning companies began with a Level 5 leader who motivated the enterprise more with inspired standards than an inspiring personality.

The executive team. The top management team, aka the executive team surrounding the CEO or business owner, needs to be proficient. The business strategy must define how the roles, power, and responsibilities are assigned, controlled, and coordinated in the organization; and how information flows among different levels of management. In their *Strategic Management* book, Carpenter and Sanders identified four criteria of an effective executive team: responds to a complex and challenging environment, manages the needs of interdependent but diverse areas, has a valuable and effective social network, and can develop a coherent plan for executive succession.

People and rewards. The people factor refers to having the right employees, developing and training them, and paying and rewarding them to accelerate the strategy implementation. In a high-performing workplace, employees not only have talent but also work well together and collaborate on ideas and resolutions. Motivated, hard-working, and talented workers generally produce better results than unmotivated, less-talented employees.

The reward system determines the compensation and promotion of people within the business. It reinforces the value and expectations, and it must align with strategy and implementation. The anonymous quote "What gets measured gets done. What gets rewarded gets done well" speaks truth.

Culture. "Culture eats strategy for breakfast" is a famous quote credited to the management guru Peter Drucker. Culture refers to the collective habits employees have formed—how they make decisions; how they respond to challenges, pressure and discomfort; and what they believe is good or bad for success. These behaviors are based on what's been incentivized, rewarded, reinforced, and possibly even punished in the workplace. The culture is practically an organization's DNA. The best time for an entrepreneur to build a great culture is in the very beginning of forming a company, "when the cement is still fluid before it gets hardened." Once a culture is formed, changing is one of the most difficult challenges a leader may face; as Torben Rick wrote, "Changing culture is a bit like changing the course of a large ship—it takes time to maneuver and whilst the engines are pushing one way, the tides and winds are pushing another." Culture's critical role will be discussed further in the Change Management chapter.

Step Three: Strategy Implementation: Learn Best Practices from the Best Practitioners

Michael Porter says, "Any strategy is only as good as its execution." Successful strategies are dependent on effective implementation, which is the process of translating ideas into actions. The three key implementation levers are (1) structure, (2) systems and processes, and (3) people and rewards. People and rewards are covered in the above Step Two, while Step Three focuses on the other two: structure and systems and processes.

Organizational structure. In their *Strategic Management* book, Carpenter and Sanders define structure as "the relatively stable arrangement of responsibilities, tasks, and people within an organization. It is the framework to divide tasks, deploy resources and coordinate departments." Big corporations adopt different basic models of organizational structures: functional, multidivisional, matrix, network, partnership, and franchise.

For startups and small businesses, establishing an organizational structure needs to be one of the top priorities. Entrepreneurs tend to build flat structures that are flexible for quick decision-making and problem solving. This involves developing fundamental processes such as defining roles and responsibilities, managerial authority, people engagement, and delegating tasks. A good organizational structure frees people to do better work, take clear ownership of projects, and drive results.

Systems and processes. Organizational systems and processes used in daily operations include budgeting, resource allocation, incentive systems, information systems, quality control, planning, and distribution. For entrepreneurs, two popular systems widely used by large corporations are worth noting: the balanced scorecard, and best practices and lean process improvement.

Balanced scorecard. First defined by Robert Kaplan and David Norton, a balanced scorecard is a performance metric used in strategic management. It measures and provides feedback in four internal categories: financial performance, customer knowledge, internal business process, and learning and growth. These categories are then broken down into specific, actionable steps on a day-to-day basis.

Traditionally, companies judge their health by how much money they make. Although vitally important, financial measures tend to focus on the short-term and only give a part of the picture. To build an organization that can stand the test of time, a more "balanced" view of performance is required. The name "balanced scorecard" comes from the idea of looking at long-term strategic measures in addition to traditional short-term financial measures. It helps guide the company to invest in the long term—in customers, employees, and innovation.

Best practices and Lean. Healthy companies are learning organizations. They relentlessly acquire and adopt best practices from both competitors and other industries to improve operations and fuel business growth. Best practices are techniques or methodologies that have proven to be most effective for optimal results. The commitment to using the best practices in any field is a signature of a vibrant company culture. People thrive in learning and doing everything better every day.

Lean is an example of best practice. It is a generic process management philosophy derived mostly from the Toyota Production System. The Japanese car manufacturer Toyota is famous for its focus on reduction of "wastes" in order to improve customer value. As discussed in the Operations Chapter, lean operations identify customer value by analyzing all the activities required to produce the products, and then optimizing the entire process from the customer's perspective. Lean drives out all waste that adds nothing to the customer. All defects, overproduction, waiting, transportation, excess inventory, motion waste, and excess processing are considered waste, since they do not add value from the viewpoint of the customers.

Also discussed in the Operations Chapter is the Lean Startup methodology, which is a practice for developing products and businesses based on "validated learning"—getting customer feedback quickly and often—and adapting and adjusting rapidly to that feedback. The objective is to eliminate uncertainty in the product development process and reduce failure.

Risk Management. Risk management identifies, avoids, and overcomes the hurdles that a strategy may encounter along the way. In the wake of the 2008 financial crisis, Robert Kaplan, a Harvard Business School professor, characterized business risks in three categories based on the degree of predictability, controllability, and management. According to his article "Risk Management and the Strategy Execution System" published in the 2009 *Harvard Business Review*, Kaplan defined three levels of risks as highlighted below.

Level 3 risks. These risks encompass routine operational and compliance risks. They are the lowest category of risks and are known and avoidable; they are, however, vital to conducting any business. Level 3 risks are closely linked to operations and processes. Examples include maintaining and updating the financial accounting and tax systems; protecting assets and information; and ensuring information security, privacy, backup, and disaster recovery. They also include the internal control processes that protect the company from fraud, negligence, legal, and other potential regulatory liabilities. These risks can be minimized by standard operating procedures, internal controls, and internal audits.

Level 2 risks. Businesses have many inherit strategy risks such as financial risk; customer, brand and reputation risk; and innovation risk. These risks are known unknowns, which can be anticipated and mitigated. For example, insurance companies can estimate the probabilities of events they insure against, including mortality, natural disasters, sickness and accidents. To prevent or mitigate level 2 risks, a business is required to identify major risks to its strategy, establish an early warning risk scorecard to signal adverse conditions when happening, and set priorities to fund prevention initiatives.

Level 1 risks. Level 1 risks refer to the unpredictable and unprecedented occurrences that create existential risk. They are difficult to predict but can be the most devastating should they occur. Such events are often referred to as "black swan" events that a business cannot control. These risks are also called global enterprise risks or the unknown/unknowns. In 2008, General

Motors and Chrysler encountered a black swan event—doubling and tripling oil prices made these two companies' large, fuel-inefficient cars unsalable, and pushed the highly leveraged companies into bankruptcy. Black swan events include natural disasters such as an earthquake, global economic phenomena such as dramatic energy price changes, regional wars, or disruptive competitors. A prior contingency plan would enable the company to act rapidly to minimize the damage when such events happen.

Risk management requires strong leadership. The CEO and business owners' ability to "see around corners," to stay true to the "why we do what we do" business purpose, and to avoid temptations—especially in good times—are sound practices in managing risks. As Kaplan pointed out, it means, "having the courage to turn down apparently profitable opportunities that expose the company to excessive risk."

Strategy vehicles to business growth. There are two types of business growth—organic and inorganic. Organic growth is the process of business expansion by increased output, customer base expansion, or new product development. Inorganic growth refers to mergers and acquisitions.

Organic growth is the most rewarding path, as it is the natural evolution of a familiar business model. Many great businesses today such as Amazon and Google started from zero with a vision and unrelenting efforts to grow from within in the beginning.

Business growth can also be generated by mergers and acquisition (M&A). However, M&A face many challenges, including cultural misfit and resistance in the acquired firm. In addition, the acquiring firms' shareholders rarely reap the benefits of acquisitions, although the wealth of the target firms' shareholders almost always increases. *BusinessWeek* reported that while 61 percent of large mergers led to shareholder losses, the average return is 4.3 percent below industry average, and 9.2 percent below S&P 500—even counting the winners. Statistics aside, M&A can be one important vehicle to achieve business expansion when used correctly.

In summary, strategies are dynamic in nature. Businesses always need to innovate and gain a competitive advantage in the fast changing world. The principle is to define a general direction, find the best people, and take massive action. Management tools such as best practices, balanced scorecards, and risk management are helpful in the implementation process. Strategy is an iterative process, and you need to frequently revisit and redefine your strategy according to shifting market conditions.

References and Suggested Readings

Carpenter, M. and W. G. Sanders. *Strategic management: Concepts.* 2nd ed. Upper Saddle River, NJ: Pearson, 2009.

Brigham, E. and M. Ehrhardt. *Financial Management: Theory and practice* 14th ed. South-Western, Cengage Learning, 2014.

Kaplan, R.S. "Risk Management and the Strategy Execution System." *Harvard Business Review.* November - December 2009.

Kaplan, R.S. and D.P. Norton. *The Balanced Scorecard: Translating Strategy into Action.* Cambridge, MA: HBR Press, 1996.

Kobulnicky, B. "Does Culture Really Eat Strategy?" *Medium.com.* https://medium.com/startup-grind/does-culture-really-eat-strategy-a3172df58912

Porter, M.E. "Competitive Advantage: Enduring Ideas and New Opportunities." *Hbs.edu.* https://www.hbs.edu/faculty/Publication%20Files/2012-0622---Rotman_Strategy_Presentation_9e4fa66e-fdbb-47dd-b03f-861f5bdc7f70.pdf

Rothaermel, F. *Strategic Management.* 3rd ed. New York, NY: McGraw-Hill, 2017.

Welch, J. & S. Welch. *Winning.* New York, NY: HarperCollins, 2005.

CHAPTER 10

LEADING CHANGE: LEADER'S ABILITY TO DRIVE CHANGE AND CULTURE

"Be open to change… You never know just how beautiful it can be." —Heather Stillufsen

In general, people resist change. We are creatures of habit. Consciously or unconsciously, we link change with uncertainty, loss of control, surprise, discomfort, self-doubt, more work, and other old unpleasant experiences. Sometimes we forget to remind ourselves, "What if it all goes right?"

The Law of Accelerating Change

Change is the constant in our physical world. Seasons change, people change, relationships change, and we change. Our human body is a master in adapting change. We go through enormous changes from a baby to an adult. In addition to the most significant change—puberty in the teen years—an adult's body is constantly in flux, replacing dead cells with new ones at the rate of 50 to 70 million a day. According to Dr. Christiane Northrup, author and medical doctor, an adult creates a whole new body every seven years, and some of the most important parts are revamped even more quickly. In the past, we have believed that genes and the contained DNAs control our destiny. But epigenetic study reveals biological mechanisms can switch genes on and off. Environment and life circumstances can cause genes to be silenced or expressed over time. In other words, the genes can be turned off (becoming dormant) or turned on (becoming active) with lifestyle changes. What you eat, where you live, who you interact with, when you sleep, how you exercise, even aging—all of these choices and factors can eventually cause chemical modifications around the genes that will turn your genes on or off over time.

The world around us is also changing rapidly. Yuval Noah Harari's book, *Sapiens, A Brief History of Humankind*, shows that our human species has gone through multiple revolutions (huge changes) in history: the cognitive revolution, the agricultural revolution, and the scientific revolution. As the *Law of Accelerating Change* works, we are witnessing yet another massive change in this data/information age that started in the late 20th century—also known as the computer age, the digital age, or the new media age. This new age is based on the interconnection of computers and portable devices such as iPads, smartphones, and the Internet of things (IoT). IoT refers to the interconnection via the Internet of computing devices embedded everywhere, enabling them to send and receive data without human interaction. Smart homes, wearable devices, connected cars, and smart refrigerators are some IoT examples. These devices connect with each other via telecommunications, so people can access information on a real-time and as-needed basis.

Every industry is in the process of transformation. The new companies in the data age tend to require fewer employees to produce the same amount of revenue and profit. If we compare General Motors (GM) as an example of the industrial age with Facebook as an example of the information age, we will find new companies need much fewer employees to operate and stay profitable. This employment disparity is the trend of the future. According to John Pugliano's book, *The Robots are Coming: A Human's Survival Guide to Profiting in the Age of Automation*, the employees at Facebook are 15 times more productive than the employees at GM when measured by profit.

The concepts of "job" and "employee" are also changing. Traditional jobs are either disappearing or changing dramatically. As the trend of automation and outsourcing accelerate in the work place, today's American employees are not only competing with workers around the world but also with robots and machines. James Altucher wrote that 94 percent of all US jobs created in the past 10 years were freelance or part-time, regardless of the political party in charge. The average income for people ages 18-35 has gone from $36,000 to $33,000 adjusted for inflation since 1992, according to the Bureau of Labor Statistics. A *Huffington Post* article in 2017 stated that artificial intelligence (AI) and other technologies could potentially eliminate one third of the US labor force, which will force people to adapt to significant changes. The kids in college now simply cannot expect to find a job for life.

The good news is one third of all job categories will expand and grow, and small companies and startups are able to perform like big companies. Mark Zuckerberg, a Harvard college dropout, can start and scale Facebook to a hundred-billion dollar company in a decade with a group of relatively inexperienced people with limited capital. This is great news to young people who have big dreams. Although only a few can succeed at the level of Zuckerberg, we can all learn to create our own employment opportunities in big or small ways. We can also find more meaningful work by following our passion. Since change is happening whether we like it or not, it is better to lead change instead of letting unwanted changes happen to us.

Are You Change-Ready?

While we are in the midst of great changes, people still fear change in general. The fear of unknown, failure, mistake, and doubt about oneself seemed to be rooted firmly in human psychology. However, these fears are just thoughts and thoughts can be changed. Franklin D. Roosevelt famously said in his 1932 inaugural address, "The only thing we have to fear is fear itself."

The book *A Course in Miracles* said, "Seek not to change the world, but choose to change your mind about the world." Indeed, the only thing we can control is our thoughts, feelings, and actions. On the one hand, change is difficult. As the Chinese proverb goes, "It's easy to change rivers and mountains but hard to change a person's nature." On the other hand, change is as easy as changing our thoughts. If we could change ourselves, the propensities in the outside world would also change—that is exactly what the quote means.

Are you willing to expand and grow your mind? Are you willing to stay on the leading edge? Life is such a great adventure when we embrace the mindset of becoming a student of life, when we develop irreplaceable skills, and when we learn to thrive in the new economy. It doesn't matter if we want to work in a business or an organization or start our own business, the best way to respond to change is to become a lifelong learner, always renewing oneself, upgrading skills and knowledge, staying open minded, and involved in leading change.

Many of us think we go to school for structured education; once we finish college, we can just have fun without the pressure of papers and exams. The truth is that after the "formal education" is over, the real education begins. We all need to be self-starters to continuously increase our knowledge, educate ourselves on new concepts and ideas in the areas of our passions and solve the problems we face.

Where do you find time to learn? Tech Crunch reported that in 2017, U.S. consumers spend 5 hours per day on mobile devices, and most of the time is spent on social media and entertainment. Thirty-five hours a week is almost a fulltime job. Imagine spending that 35 hours to learn a new skill, grow your hobby into a side business or a nonprofit to help someone or benefit a community. If we can keep learning at a rate normally associated with children or young adults, we can outgrow our peers in leading any kind of life transformation.

Twenty-five hundred years ago, the Chinese philosopher Lao Tzu said, "A journey of a thousand miles begins with a single step." To become change-ready, we can start by growing ourselves one percent better every day—physically, emotionally, intellectually, and spiritually. The compound growth will create wonders.

Process to Lead Change in a Business or an Organization

If you have worked in a company or an organization, you probably know how hard it is to initiate change and influence others. Change in the business world is complex and requires strong leadership skills. Change leaders have to face enormous resistance. The companies that failed to change have become history. Blockbuster, Blackberry, Toys 'R' Us, and Kodak were once industry leaders that were worth tens of billions of dollars, but in a matter of one or two decades, they have become irrelevant. Jack Welch said, "Change is an absolute critical part of business. You do need to change, preferably before you have to." The following section is about how to lead change in an established organization.

John Kotter, a Harvard Business School professor, is a renowned thought leader for his work on leading organizational change. His book *Leading Change* has been one of the best change management books for more than 20 years. Based on his decade-long study on more than 100 companies that attempted transformation, he concluded that companies or organizations that failed to make effective change made one or more of eight kinds of errors. These errors include: (1) too much complacency, (2) failing to create a sufficiently powerful guiding coalition, (3) underestimating the power of vision, (4) under-communicating the vision by a factor of 10 or even 1,000, (5) permitting obstacles to block the new vision,

(6) failing to create short-term wins, (7) declaring victory too soon, and (8) neglecting to anchor changes firmly in the corporate culture.

Kotter also developed a powerful framework, the famous 8-step process, based on the failures and successes he observed. In addition to recommending you read Professor Kotter's book, I'll summarize the eight-step process to help you understand the importance sequence of these steps.

1. Establishing a sense of urgency. The enemy of change is complacency. Either by human nature or lack of a major crisis, people like to maintain the status quo instead of risking unknown changes, making sacrifices, or going above and beyond the normal call of duty. To initiate a major change transformation, the leader must see the crisis or create an urgency by raising the business and customer satisfaction measure very high. The company's management and employees must honestly believe the status quo is unacceptable.
2. Creating a powerful guiding coalition. A powerful guiding coalition is a team that has the position power, expertise, credibility, accountability, leadership and teamwork to achieve the desired change. The coalition need to rally a majority of employees, 75 percent of management, and all top executives to believe that change is absolutely essential. What happens to the executives who do not believe in the change? They must leave.
3. Developing a vision and strategy. A vision is a central component of great leadership. A powerful vision paints a vivid picture of a desirable future and motivates people to make change happen. According to Kotter, a good vision has six characteristics: (1) imaginable, (2) desirable, (3) feasible, (4) focused, (5) flexible, and (6) communicable. The change leaders make sure people not only see the vision but also live

and breathe it. They also develop strategies to support and accomplish the vision.
4. Communicating the change vision. Communication needs to be done clearly and often by all levels of leadership. Effective communication in a major change initiative means that many people need to feel the urgency, understand the vision, know how to participate in it, feel committed to it, take new actions, and learn as the change unfold. Jack Welch emphasizes the importance of communication: to use every opportunity to communicate again and again until you want to puke—and then communicate some more. Often the most powerful way to communicate a new direction is through behavior. This requires the guiding coalition to walk the talk or role model the expected behavior.
5. Empowering employees for broad-based action. Major internal transformation rarely happens unless many people assist. Yet employees generally won't help or can't help, if they feel relatively powerless. Hence employee empowerment is the answer. Companies can tap into enormous employee power by removing obstacles, offering proper training, encouraging risk taking, and changing systems or structures that undermine the change vision.
6. Generating short-term wins. Major changes take time. A well-planned short-term win produces visible, unambiguous result related to the change efforts. Usually taking place during the first year or so of the change effort, a short-term win produces the following major benefits: giving evidence that people's sacrifices are worthwhile, rewarding the change leaders, providing concrete data on the change ideas, undermining cynics and resisters, keeping the bosses on board, and building credibility and momentum for long-term success.
7. Consolidating gains and producing more change. Outstanding leadership requires long-term, permanent

forward thinking. The business transformation for large companies is a huge exercise that takes years. Good leaders avoid premature declarations of victory. They use the change momentum to tackle additional and bigger changes; enroll more help from employees; promote change leaders; and transform old systems, structures and policies.

8. Anchoring changes in the corporate culture. Culture refers to norms of behavior and shared value among a group of people. It is like an iceberg: the visible part above the water is only a small portion of the whole. It is very powerful, but its near invisibility makes it hard to address directly. Culture changes only after the organization has successfully altered people's actions, after the new behavior produces some group benefits for a period of time, and after people see the connection between the new actions and the performance improvement. It comes at the end of the change process, sometimes involves changing key people and promoting people that are compatible with the new culture.

The importance of the sequence of the eight steps is to build and develop change in a natural way. Each of these steps builds on the previous one and creates the momentum to overcome enormously powerful sources of inertia.

The organization of the future. As I discussed earlier, the enterprises of the 20th century will slowly become dinosaurs if they do not adapt to the rapid change we are seeing right now. This provides an excellent opportunity for entrepreneurs to disrupt old business models and fill in the space. You need to build your future organization with a culture of persistent sense of urgency, teamwork, employee empowerment, strong communication, clean independent organizational structure, and lifelong learning—an adaptive culture that can handle the complex and changing business environment.

Even if you do not choose the entrepreneurial route,

understanding change can help you recognize those employers with cultures that have embraced change. Knowing you will most likely have multiple careers, you can plan your own education beyond formal studies. Remember to always cultivate your commitment to lifelong learning and enhance your soft skills such as leadership, communication, people management, emotional intelligence, problem solving, imagination and creativity. I encourage you to "be the change you want to see in the world" as Ghandi said.

References and Suggested Readings

Altucher, J. *Choose Yourself: Be Happy, Make Millions, Live the Dream*. Lioncrest Publishing, 2013.
Briggs, S. "How to Educate Yourself for the Future." *Opencolleges.edu.au*. http://www.opencolleges.edu.au/informed/features/how-to-educate-yourself-for-the-future/
Harari, Y.N. *Sapiens: A Brief History of Humankind*. New York, NY: HarperCollins, 2015.
Kotter, J. P. *Leading Change*. Cambridge, MA: HBR Press, 2012.
Mayberry, M. "Why You Should Strive to Be a Lifelong Learner." *Entrepreneur.com*. https://www.entrepreneur.com/article/245696

CHAPTER 11

ENTREPRENEURSHIP: HOW TO START YOUR BUSINESS

> "There are lots of bad reasons to start a company. But there's only one good, legitimate reason, and I think you know what it is: it's to change the world."
> —Phil Libin, CEO of Evernote

Every successful company was once started by an ambitious entrepreneur. "Entrepreneurs, from Henry Ford to Elon Musk, are embedded in American lore. Risk-taking and even 'irrational exuberance' together with a contrarian spirit are part of the American DNA," writes *RealClearPolicy.com*.

Entrepreneurship is essential for the improvement of the world. An entrepreneur innovates to improve our lives, create jobs, and generate wealth for themselves and our society. While we all know the "legendary garage-to-tech-titan stories" that represent the ultimate entrepreneurial success, we also see many other types of entrepreneurs and small business owners around us. These are the family owned businesses, non-profit organizations, life-style businesses, mom-preneurs, media-preneurs, and so forth. They not only create jobs but also fuel economic growth and provide social benefits. The owners enjoy the freedom that comes with being their own boss and having full control over their futures.

In Joe Vitale's book, *The Attractor Factor*, he cited a study of 1,500 people by Scrully Blotnick. The people were put into two categories: category A said they would pursue money first, and do what they really wanted to do later. Over 1,245 people were in that group. The 255 people in category B said they would seek their interests first, and trust the money would follow later. 20 years later, there were 101 millionaires from the entire 1,500 people. Only one came from group A. The remaining 100 millionaires all came from group B, the group that said that they would pursue passion first and let money come later.

Seth Godin defines entrepreneurs as those who use money (preferably someone else's money) to build a business bigger than they are. They focus on growth and on scaling the systems that they build, the more, the better. I would expand the definition of entrepreneurship to include those who generate and implement ideas, innovations or solve interesting problems that benefit society or even a small group of people.

In this chapter, we follow a typical entrepreneur's journey, walk through the stages of planning, financing, and launching a new business. We cover business plan development, market analysis, competitive positioning, business model, funding sources, company formation, intellectual property, sales, marketing, and hiring. The insights gained will give you a powerful leg up in launching either a growth or a life style business.

Are entrepreneurs born or made? You may get different answers to this question from different people. Although some entrepreneurs are born with innate abilities, many more are made by life experiences. Pat Flynn, an entrepreneur, blogger and podcaster credited his entrepreneurial success to his layoff in 2008 due to the recession. Without the layoff, he said, he would have been comfortable staying in a promising job in an architecture firm.

We are living in what James Altucher calls, "the choose yourself era," and it has never been easier to start a business than today. As the uncertainty of employment grew in most industries, more and more empowered people are exploring going out into the world, inventing, contributing—following their heart and fulfilling their dreams.

You might wonder if you have entrepreneurial traits. Jack Kaplan and Anthony Warren are both successful entrepreneurs who teach at the nation's best business schools. In their book *Patterns of Entrepreneurship Management,* they summarized the common traits of entrepreneurs as follows:

- They have the ability to deal with ambiguity.
- They are self-starters, optimists, perseverant, energetic, and action-oriented.
- They are persuasive leaders, people-oriented, natural networkers, and communicators.
- They are often creative and highly imaginative.
- They passionately seek new opportunities and are always looking for the chance to profit from change and disruption in the way business is done.
- They tolerate risk, but great entrepreneurs temper risk with reality.
- They work with urgency but balancing this with a focus on long-term goals, too.
- They focus on adaptive execution, moving forward instead of analyzing new ideas to death.
- They are open to change, not hanging on to old plans when they are not working. They pursue only the very best opportunities.

Don't worry if you don't have the traits listed; people have an enormous capacity for change. Every one of us has a unique gift that can profoundly change the world. We are all called to embark on a hero's journey in this life, and we can start with the inner work to find our true callings to adventure. If you are like me, someone who is not cut out to build a vast company like Apple, you can always choose to be the best at something: making jewelry, offering online tennis courses, starting an aftercare school, or opening a vegan restaurant that offers delicious healthy food. I want to plant the seed of "you can do it" in you. According to the research by Dr. Julian Lange, a professor of entrepreneurship at Babson College, the exposure to the ideas and lessons of entrepreneurship can have lasting effects on students, even if they are not "natural" entrepreneurs.

Alex Denoble, Professor of Management and Director of the Academic Entrepreneurship Program at San Diego State University, points out that you can't teach someone to acquire the drive, the hunger, the passion, and tenacity to pursue an entrepreneurial path. However, if someone has such "fire in their belly," they can be taught the critical entrepreneurial skills needed for the journey. The entrepreneurial process is a methodical way and consists of five stages:

1. Discovery: identify the opportunity and conduct analysis
2. Planning: develop the business plan and set up the company
3. Funding: acquire sources of funding and financial partners
4. Execution: manage the company and implement the plan
5. Scaling: scale and harvest the venture

Stage 1: Discovery: Idea and Opportunity Analysis

At the heart of every successful business is a great idea. Entrepreneurs are naturally inspired to pioneer innovations, find new or better solutions to problems, or make a difference in society. They can get their spark of an idea from the problem or pain they face, fear to eliminate, need to fulfill, or passion to pursue. They have the burning desire that urges them to see if the world also wants that idea. If you are like me, having either too many ideas or none at all, you can do two things. First, frequently ask questions as recommended by

Pat Flynn, "What are the things I do repeatedly that I don't enjoy?" "What do I enjoy the most?" "What are the things I am afraid of?" Second, follow James Altucher's suggestion to become an idea machine. Altucher makes it a requirement to write a list of 10 ideas every day, such as 10 businesses he could start or 10 blogs he could write. These ideas have made him millions in his business adventures.

From idea to vision. Entrepreneurs derive ambition and clear vision from ideas, and use vision as the lighthouse to achieve their business's goal and purpose. The Japanese proverb says, "Vision without action is a dream. Action without vision is a nightmare." Good visions make entrepreneurs dare to take action, dare to explore, dare to challenge, dare to persevere, and dare to have the determination to succeed. The life of an entrepreneur is filled with ups and downs, but vision is the source of vigor, perseverance, tenacity, and resilience.

Vision also frames the company's culture and defines "why we do what we do." Effective vision keeps everyone focused and inspired. A well-communicated and shared vision also motivates early employees and teams to work through challenging times and unites them to find innovative ways to solve difficult problems.

Good employees love to be part of something bigger than themselves—a purpose bigger than their paychecks. Southwest Airlines has a vision to become the world's most loved, most flown, and most profitable airline. It exists to connect people to what's important in their lives through friendly, reliable, and low-cost air travel. This remarkable vision encourages its employees to go the extra mile in serving customers.

Designing business models. Michael Lewis defines a business model as "how you planned to make money." It is also about how you intend to create value for your customers. A business model is the unique combination of products, services, images, and distribution that a company carries forward.

A powerful business model blends all the aspects of the business into an integrated operational system where product development, manufacturing, marketing, information, suppliers, and customers become one. The company culture plays an important role too. The culture reflects how the company treats its people and is the basis of everything every employee does.

Kaplan and Warren identified two types of tools to construct business models in their book *Patterns of Entrepreneurship Management*: the five-component model and the business model canvas. Both models answer these essential business questions:

1. Value proposition. This refers the value created for the user of the product or service. It can be a compelling story that clarifies how the customer's problem is solved, or the end-benefit of using the company's products or service.
2. Market segment. This refers to the customers the business serves. As discussed in the marketing chapter, there is an advantage for a startup to begin with a niche market, i.e., the narrow yet most valuable customers with specialized needs and characteristics. With a well-defined niche, you can focus your resources, offer the best value, and deliver the highest and most profitable sales.
3. Structure of value chain. A business is a part of a complex value chain. You must define who are the key partners, suppliers, and other stakeholders; and how to get your product or service to the customers.
4. Cost structure and profit potential. You need to understand your major costs for resources and business activities, and how you make profit.
5. Competitive strategy. Your business model needs to capture value and build competitive barriers. What is unique about what you can do better than others? How do you differentiate yourself, gain and hold advantage over others?

Opportunity and market analysis. An opportunity analysis describes how to generate sales and overcome market challenges. It analyzes customer needs and desires, market opportunity, and competition. All this forms the base of the marketing strategy.

Market research is required in this process to gather and interpret information on customer needs, preferences, issues, and the competition. It helps the company identify the viability and opportunities in the market place. Today, there are many creative ways to conduct market research through the Internet, social networks, and surveys to identify potential customers and question them about the product or service. Entrepreneur and author Ryan Levesque created "the ask method" based on his decades of experience in online businesses. It uses online surveys and quizzes to help entrepreneurs figure out the needs of the customers, know when, where and how to ask the right questions, in order to understand the pain and passions, even to uncover their language patterns. The method centers on using online techniques to discover exactly what the customers want to buy, speak the customer's language, understand the customer's problems, and define the exact segment you want to serve—and not to serve.

Opportunity analysis forms the basis of the marketing plan, which is a critical section in the business plan. This is a go-to-market exercise to clarify the business's marketing objectives and steps or actions to take in order to achieve the goals. The Marketing Chapter has covered the marketing plan in detail.

Stage 2: Planning: Develop a Business Plan and Set Up the Company

We have covered the importance of strategic planning in the Strategy Chapter. A start-up's business plan is usually the first attempt of the strategic plan. If you prepare to gain venture capital funding, a winning business plan is a must.

Most experts recommend a business plan as a twenty-five to fifty-page document to describe the business direction, goals and objectives, who is involved, why the products or services are needed by the customers, and how to implement the plan. Writing the business plan is a very valuable exercise to think through your distinctive competence and implementation. You can use the plan, whole or in part, to communicate with investors, customers, employees, and partners.

There are numerous templates available online when you Google the term "Business Plan for Startups." Kaplan and Warren's book *Patterns of Entrepreneurial Management* includes a comprehensive outline of a typical business plan with the following sections:

1. Title page and table of content
2. Executive Summary. This is a two- to three-page summary of the opportunity, problem/solution, market, and competition; why customers/consumers would choose your product or service; and forecasts financial highlights and needs. It should stand on its own to convince the investors and readers that the business will succeed.
3. Overview of the company, industry, products, and services. This section addresses the nature of the business, the customer it serves, where the company is based, and where it will do business.
4. Market analysis. This is a critical section that describes how to generate sales and overcome market challenges. Potential investors pay a lot of attention to this section. Market analysis needs to include market opportunity, competition, marketing strategy, market research, sales forecast, support material, service or product physical description, statement of use and appeal, stage of development, and testimonials from experts and prior users.
5. Marketing and sales strategy:
    a. Marketing and sales plan describes how to achieve expected sales goals.

b. Pricing strategy and plan includes the pricing method to generate profits, and distribution channels to sell the product or service.
c. Advertising, public relations, and promotion strategies describe how to inform potential customers.
d. Supporting graphics in the form of charts, graphs, and tables.
6. Operations. This section provides a detailed operation plan. Depending on the nature of the business, it needs to cover product/service development, manufacturing, supply chain, quality, maintenance, and support.
7. Management team. This section includes the team's talents and skills, organization chart, policy and strategy for employees, the board of directors, and the advisory board. If you are going to attract potential investors, you need to inform them of the distinctive advantages your team has. As the saying goes, "Businesses don't fail, people fail businesses." People are one of the most important factors investors consider.
8. Financial plan. This section requires a credible, comprehensive set of projections of the anticipated financial performance. It must include a set of assumptions, projected income statement, projected cash flow statement, current balance sheet, and other financial information.
9. The amount of funds required. This section describes how much money is required to finance the business, where the funds will be spent, and when they will be needed. The use of funds can be in the areas of research and development, purchase of assets or equipment, and working capital.
10. Exhibits. This section typically includes census data and other statistics, market potential, operation process flow, and detailed financials.

A business plan is essential in launching a new business. Although developing the plan is time consuming, the effort and exercise you go through to collect information on the market, operations and financials are extremely valuable. A comprehensive and well-written business plan is mandatory if you want to raise funds from outside investors.

Setting up the company

One of the most important business decisions is to choose a legal structure for your business. Common types of business structures and corporations include: sole proprietorship, C-corporation, S-corporation, limited liability company (LLC), and partnership. The legal form of the business should be determined based on your short-term and long-term needs, as each structure has different implications in the areas of tax, liability, cost, and the need for outside investors.

Sole proprietorship is the simplest form of business. It means a single owner does business alone and requires only a state or city business license to open. This is a simple way to initiate business with low start-up fees. Since there is no separation of personal assets and business assets, the drawback is that you are personally liable for business debt and legal problems. The pros and cons of sole proprietorships are depicted in the table below:

Advantages	Disadvantages
• Easy to form, operate and discontinue • Owner keeps all profit after debts are paid • Total decision-making authority • No legal restrictions	• Owner remains personally liable for lawsuits filed against the business • Limited access to capital • Limited skills and capabilities of the sole owner

C-corporation or C-corp is an independent legal entity under state laws, separate from the people who own, control, and manage it. A C-corp can conduct business, sign contracts, pay taxes, sue, and be sued. It is the most common form of business ownership.

A C-corp can have many owners. The owners of a C-corp hold shares of stock in the corporation, which represents a percentage of ownership. The officers and directors of the corporation conduct the actual business.

A C-corp does not dissolve when its owners (shareholders) change or die, and the owners have limited liability—that is, they are not personally responsible for the corporation's debts or law suits. Sole proprietary and partnership companies can convert into a C-corp when needed.

C-corp is the most appropriate structure if a business needs to raise a large sum of money (such as from Venture Capital firms) to capitalize on fast growth and opportunities, or plan an IPO in the future. The pros and cons of C-corp are:

Advantages	Disadvantages
• Limited liability of the shareholders, with legal protection of personal assets. • Ability to attract and raise capital—it is a structure that venture capitalists require • No limit to the number of shareholders, and shareholders are the owners of the business. • Transferrable ownership. • Access to skills, expertise, and knowledge.	• Cost and time involved in the incorporation process. • Double taxation—both corporation profits and shareholder dividends are taxed • High administration compliance costs • Corporate governance rules to follow • Directors held accountable

S-corporation or S-corp is a closely held corporation (in some cases, a limited liability company or a partnership) that elects to pass corporate income, losses, deductions, and credit through to their shareholders for federal tax purposes. Shareholders of S-corps report the flow-through of income and losses on their personal tax returns, and are assessed tax at their individual income tax rates. This allows S-corps to avoid double taxation on the corporation income. The IRS has strict requirements regarding the qualification of S-corp status as described on its website. The pros and cons of S-corp are:

Advantages	Disadvantages
- Limited liabilities for the owners - Enjoys corporation status, but owners pay taxes. - Suitable for start-ups anticipating net losses, or high profitable firms with substantial dividends payout to shareholders.	- Strict rules to maintain S-corp status; breaking them lead to disastrous tax consequences. - Administration and cost burdens to qualify S-corp

Partnership is usually defined as an association of two or more people carrying on as co-owners of a business for profit. Doctors, lawyers, architects, and accountants typically form partnership businesses.

There are two types of partnerships. The first is a general partnership, which requires that each partner participate in all profits and losses equally or on an agreed-upon ratio. Normally, a general partner has unlimited liability, which includes personal assets outside of business association. The second is a limited partnership, which limits the liability of the partners to the extent of their capital contributions. A limited partner must have at least one general partner's personal assets at stake. The general partner in this case can be a corporation, so only the corporate assets are liable. The pros and cons of partnership are:

Advantages	Disadvantages
• Easy to establish and operate • Complimentary skills of partners • Division of profits • Larger pool of capital • No double taxation, owners report their share of profit and loss of the company on their personal tax returns. • Flexible in decision making and attracting limited partners as investors	• Unlimited liability of at least one partner – the general partner • Limitations and restrictions in raising capitals • Restrictions to eliminate for the general partnership • Lack of continuity if one partner dies. • Potential for personality and authority conflicts

Limited liability company (LLC) is a blend of some of the best characteristics of corporations, partnerships, and sole proprietorships. An LLC is like a corporation in terms of limited liability, and is like a partnership regarding the flexibility to divide profit among owners. An LLC can elect to be treated either as a partnership or as a corporation for federal income tax purposes. The pros and cons of an LLC are:

Advantages	Disadvantages
• Owners do not assume liabilities for debt • Not a tax-paying entity (tax benefits pass through to members) • No restrictions on the number and types of owners • Statutory meetings are not required • Can be converted to a C-corporation	• Venture capitalists usually do not invest in an LLC • Cannot take the company public (no IPO) • Restrictions on transfer of ownership • Management and member rules are different in each state

Both sole proprietorships and LLCs can be converted to C-corporations, with the help of a business lawyer. Ultimately, there is no single solution that works for every type of business. The choice really depends on the type of business, the owners, and business growth goals.

Stage 3: Funding: Acquire Sources of Capital

A start-up company can raise funding in many ways. Two distinctive types of funding are available at different growth stages of a company: early stage funding and equity funding. Most entrepreneurs start their companies with self-funding or bootstrapping, which means relying on little capital from their own existing resources. Raising money from external investors generally means losing control of the company. Equity investors such as venture capitalists provide funding to companies in exchange for part ownership in the form of shares. Therefore, the control of the company is an important decision an entrepreneur has to make when starting a business. If control of the company is the main objective, then self-funding and bootstrapping must be used. If on the other hand, you plan to acquire significant personal wealth, and are comfortable with trading control, then seeking outside investors is the route to go.

Early stage funding. Early stage funding includes self-funding, bootstrapping, family and friends, angels, factoring and supplier lines of credit, micro-equity and micro-loans, personal loans, incubators, and government grants. Most entrepreneurs are experts at using various bootstrapping methods or self-financing through retained profits from sales before they can acquire equity or bank loans. The longer the entrepreneur can survive without selling ownership, the greater the value that will be retained.

The common wisdom is: before you think about raising funds

from outside parties, find your first customer and make sure your product or service delights the customer. Money will come. In addition, it usually takes twice as long as anticipated to raise money externally, so you need to plan ahead and not let financial requirements be a surprise. Here are the highlights of popular sources:

1. Self-funding. Self-funding is a necessary stage as the majority of new businesses are started with funds that come from personal savings or various forms of the personal equity of the founder(s). Personal investment also includes "sweat equity," which means owners either donate their time or provide it at below market value to get the business established. Investors and lenders alike expect the owner(s) to put some of their own assets at risk; i.e., put some "skin in the game."
2. Bootstrapping. Bootstrapping means to finance a new company through seeking the help or input from others—friends, family, colleagues, and stakeholders such as suppliers, customers, the public, and unions. For example, the business can negotiate payment terms with suppliers to pay 90 days or 180 days, so it has time to collect cash from customers before paying the suppliers.

    Some other bootstrapping techniques include: no or low rent, which means using one's residence for office or workspace; bartering for goods and services; negotiating an advance from a customer or strategic partner; negotiating with manufacturers on financing agreements; trading intellectual property rights or services; renting or leasing equipment; buying used equipment; accessing university and government labs for more expensive equipment; asking suppliers' and customers' help; joining a start-up incubator or accelerator; joining cooperative purchases such as buyers' club to save health insurance costs; outsourcing payroll,

bookkeeping, and tax return services; and using credit card debt when bank loans or equity options are not available.
3. Family and friends. This is a very popular source for start-up capital. However, even with family and friends, you should always document the disclosure of important information about the venture, the company's risks, and financial requirements.
4. Business incubators. These are usually facilities established to nurture young startup firms during their early months or years. They provide affordable space, shared offices and services, hands-on management training, mentoring, and seed funding.
5. Government funding. Federal, state, and local governments have a range of programs to support early stage companies. These are federal, state, and local small business finance initiatives and innovation research grants. States and local governments also have small business assistance programs through loans, tax benefits, subsidized rents, or small business incubators.

Federal agencies such as the Small Business Administration (SBA) (www.sba.org) provide information about sources of loans and other helpful information on starting and managing a small business. The Small Business Innovation Research Program (SBIR) supports scientific excellence and technological innovation through the investment of Federal research funds (SBIR.gov). A startup can participate in the competitive SBIR funding programs. The Small Business Technology Transfer Program (STTR) is another program similar to SBIR, while STTR is the expansion of the public/private sector partnership to include joint venture opportunities for small businesses and nonprofit research institutions. There are also other funding sources for small businesses that are 51 percent or more owned by minorities or women.

6. Angel investors. The ABC reality show *Shark Tank* is the dramatized version of angel investors. Angel investors are high-net-worth individuals who have funds and are willing to risk those funds in start-up companies. This can be an excellent source of raising early-stage capital if self-funding and friends are not viable. Angels usually invest their own money, in the range of $50,000 to $500,000 to get a company started, and they expect 20 to 35 percent of return on their investment. The best way to reach out to angel investors is through word of mouth such as referral from friends and acquaintances, local chambers of commerce, and networking with local groups of entrepreneurs.
7. Micro-equity. Some angel investors form regional networks of advisers. An entrepreneur can submit an idea to qualify for micro-equity. For a small percentage ownership of the company, they provide cash to develop business plans or product prototypes. They also introduce the founders to a bigger network of angel investors, potential employees, attorneys, bankers, and venture capitalists, all of whom can help prepare for the first round of investment.
8. Micro-loan. A micro-loan provides a small amount of funds to a new business. These are short-term loans for working capital or the purchase of inventory, supplies, furniture, fixtures, machinery, and equipment. For example, the SBA in the U.S. offers an average of $13,000 micro-loans for certain types of business, up to $50,000.
9. Bank loan. Bank loan is a type of debt financing, and the loan must be paid back with interest and may require the owner's personal guarantee on part of or all of the money. The main advantage is the owner does not have to give up any part of ownership to receive the funds. Business counselors usually advise entrepreneurs to develop a relationship with local banks early on, which can come in handy when the company grows and needs money.

10. Factoring and supplier funding. These are alternatives to bank loans. Some private lenders offer funds for a business operation by using purchase orders from reputable customers as security for the loan. Sometimes suppliers may also give the company a line of credit in exchange for purchase orders.

Equity funding. Venture capital (VC) is the most common source of equity funding for high-growth and high-potential startups. Capital from equity funding is acquired in exchange for a share of business ownership. There are several stages of equity funding:

- Seed funding. The seed stage is the first phase in raising outside capital, usually from angel investors, angel groups or early-stage VCs. The basic requirement is the business needs to be in a good market with a good product to satisfy that market. These early investors can provide business wisdom and network connections in addition to funding.
- Early/growth stage, which is usually called series A. The name is given to a company's first significant round of venture capital financing. Series A refers to the class of preferred stock sold to investors in exchange for their investment.
- Expansion stage funding, which is usually called series B or series C/D. Very few companies make it to this stage, as it requires the business to grow month after month, with significant revenue in the millions of dollars.
- Mezzanine round. This is the final phase of funding in preparation for an IPO or acquisition.

The process of choosing a VC partner is a two-way street. While the VC evaluates the business, the entrepreneur also needs to thoroughly research the VC to make sure it is the right fit for the business. An entrepreneur typically works closely with VC partners for five to 10 years, so it is wise to pick a partner with expertise, credibility, and a matching personality. Jack Welch says there is plenty of money out there, and money is always looking for great ideas and entrepreneurs with big dreams and big ambitions.

Crowdfunding. Crowdfunding is a way to source funding for a venture (or project) by raising small amounts of money from a large number of people, typically through websites such as Kickstarter, Indiegogo or GoFundMe. Crowdfunding platform generates lightning-speed startup funding, offers instant feedback, helps the company sell to early customers, and builds a fan base. For example, Indiegogo is a popular site for entrepreneurial projects. Sondors is one of the extraordinary startups that sold over $6 million worth of electric bikes on Indiegogo.

Liquidity event. A liquidity event allows founders and early investors to convert some or all of their ownership shares into cash. This is typically done either in the sale of the company (the most usual way) or through an IPO, which allows shareholders to sell shares to the public. Ownership in a private company has real value only when a liquidity event occurs.

Stage 4. Execution: Building the Company

In this stage of building a long-lasting company, all the executive MBA principles and practices covered in this book matter: leadership, communications, financial management, people management, strategy, marketing, and operations. They are the building blocks of a successful business.

A startup is young and fragile, and it is important that an entrepreneur manage two key resources—people and cash. Human resources and financial practices are the two essential elements; all other areas are built upon these two. Chapters Four and Five cover the basics of these subjects, and I encourage you to expand and learn further in each area. Remember, a great company is by design, not by chance.

People. This is the most likely factor to determine a startup's success or failure. A company is usually started by one or a few committed people who have the vision and the commitment to see it through to success. On the people management level, finding and hiring the most capable people that fit the company culture is one of the most important things the entrepreneur can do as a leader.

An entrepreneur must have the ability to articulate and communicate a vision clearly and effectively to employees and investors. The company culture is based on the vision but is reflected by every day interaction with employees—how the company hires, fires, celebrates, compensates, and values. On the other hand, clear guidelines and procedures for dealing with conflict of interest and ethical transgressions also help build and sustain a company's culture. Kaplan and Warren listed these key attributes of a successful innovative company: honesty, alignment, risk, teamwork, empowerment, freedom, support, engagement, stimuli, and communication.

Cash flow. Poor cash management practice is believed to be the number one reason why businesses go bankrupt. "Cash is king" is an age-old saying. The initial goal is to stay alive until the startup can nail the secret formula for success. I have personally witnessed promising technology startups run out of cash, lay off workers, and shut down before they had the time to establish a strong customer base in the market place.

Good financial management practices and tools can do the following: track and analyze the company's performance, manage day-to-day cash flows, budget and forecast future cash needs, aid in investment decisions, prepare financial statements (the balance sheet, the income statement, and the statement of cash flows) for investors and lenders, and prepare tax filing.

Building a successful company is a marathon, not a sprint. Successful entrepreneurs keep their eyes set on the future, but take concrete small steps in the daily operations, navigating through success, mistakes, and crisis. Although they might plan to sell the company in the future, in the present moment they focus on building a solid business by solving the problem or pain of the customers, building something they are passionate about, and creating a story that they are proud to tell their children and grandchildren.

Stage 5. Scaling: Scale and Harvest the Venture

Scale (or scale up) is to grow and expand a business to a larger market position in a profitable way. Scale is about adding revenue at a rapid rate while adding resources at an incremental rate. Every big company was a startup at some point. Exceptional entrepreneurs like Bill Gates and Jeff Bezos can start a business and grow with the business, but many struggle. According to *Harvard Business Review* article "Why Entrepreneurs Don't Scale," scaling a business requires different sets of skills and habits, and requires the entrepreneur to switch from a business development to an executive mode. "Leaders who scale do so because they take deliberate steps to confront their shortcomings and become the leaders their organizations need them to be."

The Leadership Chapter in this book provides the framework for entrepreneurs who are growing out of the startup mode. It is worth repeating what an effective leader does: recruit, develop and retain an executive team and employees; develop vision and strategy for the growing business; form a great adaptive culture; and communicate vision and strategy throughout the business. A leader that walks the talk can gain trust from employees and make employees feel safe, be willing to innovate, create, take risks and stretch themselves. Successful leaders also work with trusted mentors and coaches from both inside and outside the organization for feedback and growth. They are self-motivated lifelong learners and avid readers, so they keep an open mind to change, evolve and grow themselves.

Harvesting and exiting the venture. An exit strategy refers to the intent to "cash out" an investment made by the business owner(s) and investors (such as venture capitalists). No matter you are building a billion-dollar company or running a family business, the most common exit strategies are: selling the business, selling an equity stake to a strategic partner, merging with another business, or going public by issuing an IPO. Some businesses choose to sell the company to its managers (MBO—management buy-out), employees (ESOP—employee stock ownership plan), or family members. Each of these options has pros and cons; the business owner must weigh the options and make the best decision.

VC firms require an exit route to realize the return on their investment by converting their investment back to cash. For VC backed businesses, there are usually three exit strategies, also called liquidity events: selling the company (most common), IPO, or management buyout.

Shaping your harvest strategy is a complicated task that requires a clear vision and good planning. The right exit strategy completes the entrepreneurial lifecycle, protects and builds wealth, and ensures the business has a smooth transition and a long-lasting legacy.

Final Word for the Non-Traditional Entrepreneur: Be the Master of Your Own Fate

You may have this question in your mind: "What if I am not made to be an entrepreneur, or what if I choose not to be an entrepreneur?" Very few of us are born to become entrepreneurs like Jeff Bezos, but we all have to be the masters of our own fate in this rapidly changing world. To those of you who are still in school or college when you read this book, the future will be vastly different than the previous generations. Current popular jobs such as teachers, lawyers, doctors, pharmacists, accountants, bookkeepers, tax advisors, auditors, real estate agents, drivers, retail clerks, manufacturing and construction jobs will mostly if not completely be replaced by robots, AI, and machines.

I believe the future for human beings will be bright. What if we don't have to go to those meaningless 9-5 jobs? What if we all could do what we love and make a living around that? What if we could all be happy, healthy, and fulfilled by living from our passion without other people bossing us?

The answer is You Can! You can earn an income by following your dreams and do what you love every single day for the rest of your life. Seth Godin is the author/entrepreneur who wrote the book *Tribes: We Need You to Lead Us*. He defines tribes as a unique group of fans, friends, and followers who resonate with your worldview. Godin noted you can make a living with 1,000 true fans. You can start your own tribe, which is a gathering of people who share the same passion as a craftsperson, musician, designer, author, and all walks of life. There are entrepreneurs who build successful online businesses by designing clothes for dolls, selling course plans for elementary school librarians, or teaching people how to draw cartoons. All of these entrepreneurs started their own tribes, shared personal, relevant and anticipated messages, and built trust with their members. Money comes as a result of trust and shared passion.

Remember that great marketing definition by Joe Vitale? "Marketing is finding the target audience who most wants and welcomes your products or service." That audience already has the mindset to look for your product or service; the sales transaction is just a natural match. Here are just some examples of passion business:

Shultz Photo School. Kyle Shultz is a dad of three lovely children. He takes beautiful wedding photos. After being asked by many people on how to take better pictures, he started the Shultz Photo School to help parents do exactly that—take better pictures. With close to 90,000 parents who are in his tribe, he was able to build a passion business doing what he loves—taking priceless pics of kids and other memorable moments.

Charity: Water. Scott Harrison started Charity:Water, a non-profit organization providing clean, safe drinking water to people in developing nations. During his volunteer work in Africa, he noticed that most of the diseases were caused by unsafe water and poor sanitation. He founded Charity:Water and uses 100 percent of all public donation to fund water projects, while private donors cover the costs of his non-profit operations. The organization has raised hundreds of millions of dollars since 2006. The website (charitywater.org) says more than seven million people get clean water through close to 25,000 water projects in 25 countries. Imagine the impact he has had on other people's lives!

Entrepreneur on Fire (EOF). John Lee Dumas founded EOF by doing a daily podcast that features the story of a successful entrepreneur. He is a "media-preneur" who produces his own daily "30-minute radio show" at home by interviewing entrepreneurs. He grew his business into a multi-million dollar entity, while inspiring entrepreneurs and business owners around the world. He has total transparency and authenticity, publishes his monthly income, and lets his audience learn from his successes and failures.

Dr. John Yang, the dean of the Beijing International MBA program at Beijing University, says: "In my opinion, entrepreneurship is a matter of the heart, and education is a matter of the brain. It is difficult to teach a heart." These examples show that you can make a living with your heart by connecting people and giving them a place in the world. The pleasant side effect is when you do it right, making money happens.

References and Suggested Readings

Altucher, J. "10 New Reasons You Have to Quit Your Job In 2017." *Jamesaltucher.com*. http://www.jamesaltucher.com/2017/03/quit-your-job-2017/

Godin, S. "Tribes Q&A." Inspired by the book *Tribes: We Need You to Lead Us*. http://sethgodin.typepad.com/seths_blog/files/TribesQA2.pdf

Hamm, J. "Why Entrepreneurs Don't Scale?" *Hbr.org.* https://hbr.org/2002/12/why-entrepreneurs-dont-scale

Howes, L. How to Build Your Business Around Your Passion (and Why Most Never Do). *Lewishowes.com.* https://lewishowes.com/entrepreneur/business-and-passion/

Kaplan, J. M. and A. C. Warren. *Patterns of entrepreneurship Management.* 4th ed. Hoboken, NJ: John Wiley & Sons, Inc., 2013.

Ottino, J.M. & M. P. Mills. "Have We Reached Peak Entrepreneurship?" *Realclearpolicy.com.* http://www.realclearpolicy.com/articles/2017/03/07/have_we_reached_peak_entrepreneurship_110183.html

CHAPTER 12

CAPSTONE: LEADING AS A CEO AND A BUSINESS OWNER

> "A leader is one who knows the way, goes the way, and shows the way."
> —John C. Maxwell, American author, speaker, and pastor

Thank you for reading this book to this final chapter, in which we take a holistic view of how each of the MBA tools fit together. The Executive MBA Capstone course centers around a project that requires the student to use the knowledge and research skills learned from the entire MBA experience to practice leading a company or solve a real world business problem. It requires the student to have the mindset of a CEO or a business owner; and use the correct leadership skills, principles and practices. It utilizes the key management concepts such as strategic thinking and execution, building a dynamic culture, people management, financial management, communication and presentation, and change management. We have covered these topics in the previous chapters, and I invite you to explore each area through continuous learning, reading, doing, reflection and improvement cycle.

Aileen Yi Fan

How Do MBA Tools Work Together?

You do not need an Executive MBA (EMBA) degree, but you need the EMBA equivalent knowledge and tools to succeed in leading a business, mitigate risk, and increase the probability of success. Education comes in many forms, and the knowledge you learn from an EMBA can also be learned through a job with the necessary growing opportunities or simply start your own business and learn as you go. For example, if you plan to start a tech company, you can go work for a tech start-up and learn; you can hire a mentor who is already successful in your area; or you can learn (sometimes the hard way) from your own success and failure. No matter how you plan to learn, you need to master the following essential knowledge and skills to build a successful business.

- Leadership. John Maxwell says, "Everything rises and falls on leadership." Leaders inspire action and adaptability in an unpredictable world. Leaders help people improve, grow, thrive, and succeed. Leadership starts with leading yourself, which means knowing your own inspiration, purpose, goal, and direction. Leadership can be nurtured through commitment to lifelong learning, and working toward becoming a better person every day. It can be cultivated by strengthening your emotional intelligence, and learning and practicing leadership principles, concepts, tools, and skills.
- Communication. All good leaders are good communicators, and do so with candor and integrity. As James Humes puts it, "The art of communication is the language of leadership." Effective communication helps you inform, inspire, persuade, and engage people to fulfill business goals and objectives. Employees who share the same goal achieve better results and take good care of customers.
- People management. Sir Richard Branson's formula for success: "Find the people smarter than you, getting them to

work at your business, giving them the great work, making it fun, and stepping back and leaving them alone, so you can focus on your vision." Your ability to select, develop, promote, and manage the right people is the most important factor for success. It is a practice of both art and science to hire the right players, manage your human resources, and implement a proper compensation and reward system to achieve your desired results.
- Strategy. Strategy helps you plan for the future by defining the organization's resources and capabilities and formulating a winning execution. As Jack Welch puts it, "Find a general direction (the key things that set you apart either through a differentiated or low-cost strategy) and implement like hell."
- Marketing. You need to understand what makes customers buy what you are selling. Marketing involves a range of activities to convey a persuasive message to a target audience who most welcome your product or service. The marketing activities include but are not limited to market research, customer value and psychology, product positioning, pricing, branding, and advertising through various channels with which your customers interact.
- Finance. Financial accounting is the "language of business." Leaders must learn to speak with numbers and have a clear understanding of financial concepts, principles, and tools. Understanding financial data will enable you to confidently make decisions based on the numbers and reports. In addition, financial management skills help you analyze and understand the qualities that investors seek in a company.
- Operations management. All businesses come down to delivering high quality products and services efficiently to their customers. Operations are the processes and practices that make all things happen at the highest level of efficiency. It includes areas such as quality management, supply chain, logistics, project management, scheduling, organizational

design, talent management, and continuous process improvement.
- Change management. Powerful forces such as technology and globalization are constantly changing the business landscape. Although most people resist change by nature, leaders recognize the need for change, willingly embrace change, and know how to lead change. To lead change effectively, you need to commit yourself to lifelong learning; be the change you want to see in the world; and learn to drive change through authentic leadership, persuasive communication, collaboration, energy and passion.
- Entrepreneurship. If you are inspired to be an entrepreneur, you need to learn the stages of planning, financing, and launching a new business. The entrepreneurial process includes business plan development, market analysis, competitive positioning, business models, funding sources, company formation, trade secrets and intellectual property, sales, marketing, and hiring. Although not everyone is inspired to be an entrepreneur, you can still work for yourself in myriad ways. It has never been easier to start your own small passion business. The freedom of making your own decisions, controlling your own time, and exploring your own ideas can be very empowering.

Critical Life Skills For the Future

The world around us is changing at an accelerated speed. A job as we know it will soon be an outdated industrial age relic. Most educational systems, however, are still designed for the industrial age, producing reasonably well-educated workers and employees for a corporation or factory. However, AI, machines, and robots are transforming every single industry from healthcare, education, transportation, finance, retail to manufacturing. We have seen robot-operated factories, robot-operated banks, no-clerk supermarkets, and robotic therapist conducting millions of conversations a week with patients. Yuval Noah Harari is a historian, professor, and author of international bestsellers. In his book *Homo Deus, A Brief History of Tomorrow,* he warns that workplace automation and AI could leave humans jobless and useless, both economically and politically. Harari says what you learn in school or college may be irrelevant by the time you turn 40 or 50, so you will have to reinvent yourself again and again, and faster and faster.

Change-proof skills. Despite these dire predictions, we all have enormous capacity for change. We can develop future-proof skills in cognitive, creative, and emotional areas. I encourage you to cultivate these critical life skills for the future: authentic leadership, critical thinking, complex problem solving, listening, decision making, mental elasticity, imagination, original ideas, collaboration, open-mindedness, flexibility, creativity, willingness to re-invent yourself, and emotional intelligence—self-awareness, self-regulation, motivation, empathy, and social skills.

Science and art skills. Future problem solving will require interdisciplinary knowledge. For example, an organ or body part creator will need knowledge in biology, genetics, and biomedical engineering. The current hot areas of science, technology, engineering and math (STEM), coding, social, mobile, analytics and cloud (SMAC) will continue to be important skills you can master if you have the passion in these areas.

Art sparks imagination, makes life joyful, and influences society's opinions and values. Arts education nurtures essential skills such as creativity, critical thinking, and cultural awareness. Even if you plan to focus on STEM study, you can still choose a subject in music, literature, dance, theatre and visual arts to enhance creativity and appreciate life more.

Personal life skills. Most school systems do not teach the most important factors that affect your personal life: health, nutrition and fitness; joyous relationship and parenting; character building such as self-responsibility and good habits; personal finance; and quality of life. These are the skills to build a successful and happy life. You must take the initiative to educate yourself.

Lifelong learner and personal growth. The business school I studied at is a top online business school; the students are working adults who strive to improve their knowledge and skills for better work and personal fulfillment. We had a slogan: learn on Monday, apply on Tuesday, and see results on Friday. It is a constant learn–apply–result–reflect–improve cycle that enriched our learning experience tremendously. From that experience, I have made a conscious decision to be a lifelong learner—an ongoing, voluntary, and self-motivated person in pursuit of knowledge, skills, and wisdom.

If Harari's predictions are true, what you learn from your college education will be outdated almost overnight, and you will need to reinvent yourself faster and faster to understand the world and remain relevant. So the ability to "learn how to learn" is one of the greatest skills you can master. Commit yourself to becoming a lifelong learner even after your formal schooling. It will enhance your understanding of the world, improve the quality of your life, spark new ideas, and recognize opportunities to solve the world's problems.

Imagine and dream big. As demonstrated by Mark Zuckerberg and Facebook, it is now possible for a group of relatively inexperienced people with limited capital to succeed on a large scale. We can all dream big. As the founder of AOL Steve Case says, "You shouldn't focus on why you can't do something, which is what most people do. You should focus on why perhaps you can, and be one of the exceptions."

I believe the future will be wonderful for human beings. Imagine a future in which we are paid to play, create, learn, and grow. Imagine a future in which we have the choice to engage in things we love, have fun, and work from inner motivation. Imagine a future in which we are driven by our mission and passion to pursue happiness, growth, peace, and abundance. With our collective efforts, we can make it happen.

Live from Your Life Purpose and Passion

Joseph Campbell said, "A hero is someone who has given his or her life to something bigger than oneself." I want to encourage you to embark on your own hero's journey. We're all here for a reason, and we're all called to a specific purpose in life; too often, however, we just follow what everybody else is doing, losing sight of that purpose because we're so entrenched by all the dramas that we encounter every day. Money becomes an obstacle, and desires get put on the backburner so that we can focus on responsibilities and obligations. And before we know it, we're no longer living the life we want. We are simply going through the motions, doing what society/parents/peers have told us we are supposed to do. We become so scared of exploring the world beyond what we are comfortable of knowing, just like the big domiciled elephant that is tied by a small rope. The elephant could, at any time, break away from the rope it was tied to, but it refuses to do so.

We are all naturally motivated by honorable missions and personal growth. Each of us has a unique gift that can profoundly change the world. Your internal strength is what eventually gives you the vision, confidence, independence, energy, passion, curiosity, tenacity, and resilience to embrace life's uncertainties and risks. You are so much more extraordinary than you were made to believe. Connect to your passion and source, and become the "master of your fate and captain of your soul."

Mark Twain famously said, "Twenty years from now, you will be more disappointed by the things that you didn't do than by the ones you did do, so throw off the bowlines, sail away from safe harbor, catch the trade winds in your sails. Explore, Dream, Discover."

References and Suggested Readings

Greer, S. "Does an Entrepreneur Need an MBA?" *Hbr.org*. https://hbr.org/2010/11/does-an-enterpreneur-need-an-m

Groysberg, B. "The Seven Skills You Need to Thrive in the C-Suite." *Hbr.org*. https://hbr.org/2014/03/the-seven-skills-you-need-to-thrive-in-the-c-suite

Smaple, I. "AI Will Create 'Useless Class' of Human, Predicts Bestselling Historian." *Theguardian.com*. https://www.theguardian.com/technology/2016/may/20/silicon-assassins-condemn-humans-life-useless-artificial-intelligence

Westernberg, J. "Why now is the best time in human history to be an entrepreneur." *Businessinsider.com*. http://www.businessinsider.com/now-is-the-best-time-to-be-an-entrepreneur-2016-1

ABOUT THE AUTHOR

Do you face parenting challenges as the world's media promotes fear and insecurity every day? Do you want to teach your children to face an ever-changing world and still have the courage to embark on their heroes' journey? As a fellow mother, Aileen Yi Fan invites you to join this adventure, to teach ourselves and our kids to lead our own lives and businesses.

Aileen is a committed lifelong learner, and an advocate for change. She is the owner of a boutique marketing and public relations agency serving small businesses. She studied biomedical engineering and business administration. Throughout her 22 years of corporate career before starting her own business, Aileen worked at Fortune 50, 500, mid-size public-traded companies, and start-ups in three countries: China, Canada and the U.S. During her recent executive MBA study, Aileen learned the most valuable leadership principle—to be a change leader and take total responsibility in all aspects of her life—health, finance, career, relationship and personal growth. She hopes by sharing her life experiences and lessons, some like-minded people can gather, learn, and inspire each other. Aileen is a proud mom of two beautiful children, Ian and Amy. They inspire her to be the best version of herself, and to make a little progress every day—physically, emotionally, intellectually, and spiritually.

www.ingramcontent.com/pod-product-compliance
Lightning Source LLC
Chambersburg PA
CBHW020651220526
45464CB00001B/392